DEVOTIONS T(
YOUR SPIRIT & F⌐⌐⌐ ⌐⌐⌐⌐ ⌐⌐⌐ FAITH

WHO WILL YOU BE
IN THE MIDST OF
your storm?

DEVOTIONS TO STRENGTHEN
YOUR SPIRIT & FUEL YOUR FAITH

WHO WILL YOU BE
IN THE MIDST OF
your storm?

VIRGINIA C. DENMARK

LIFEWISE BOOKS

WHO WILL YOU BE IN THE MIDST OF YOUR STORM?

Devotions to Strengthen Your Spirit & Fuel Your Faith

VIRGINIA C. DENMARK

All scriptures are taken from the KING JAMES VERSION (KJV): KING JAMES VERSION, public domain.

Published by:

⚙ LIFEWISE BOOKS

PO BOX 1072
Pinehurst, TX 77362
LifeWiseBooks.com

To contact the author: virginiadenmark.com

ISBN (Print): 978-1-952247-50-7
ISBN (Ebook): 978-1-952247-51-4

Blessed be God, even the Father of our Lord Jesus Christ, the Father of mercies, and the God of all comfort; Who comforteth us in all our tribulation, that we may be able to comfort them which are in any trouble, by the comfort wherewith we ourselves are comforted of God.

(2 CORINTHIANS 1:3-4)

table of contents

INTRODUCTION

I'm so excited you are reading this book because I KNOW God has something special for you within these pages. I can say this because God confirmed in one night of destruction that my faith walk had made the devil mad. I began writing when I was still in a period of deep grief and loss, and it took nearly two years to realize it was less about me and more about others—like you! On the first day of 2017, I committed to leading out in a church Bible study beginning in February. It was so positively received by that precious group that afterward I stood outside and praised God underneath the shadowy canopy of trees in my yard. Within forty-five minutes, though, that excitement turned to terror as a tornado—in Florida—touched down in my yard and uprooted and splintered almost all of the old oaks and pines where I had only minutes before stood in awe of God.

While my family was safe, my yard was destroyed and the roof was damaged. The storm was so loud our son could barely hear us yelling for him to run to the safe place in the center of our home; his guitars on the wall were rattling, and the tornado was headed directly toward us like a train—and we were sitting in the path on the tracks. But God! He placed His hands over our home protecting us from the storm. We were safe, yet the next morning revealed the full damage done to our yard. While the reality was devastating, it was also one of the best days I had in years, because the storm reassured me I was in God's perfect will. Eyeing the debris, my husband said to me, "Keep praying!" My reply? "You betcha!"

This book survived that storm for YOU.

During much of my life, I have encouraged others to reach for bigger visions. But that was not where God was to leave me. He wanted to take me deeper because I was not called to be a cheerleader but instead to be a "broken-builder" for those who have experienced loss, grief, and trials that may have taken them down into a pit. Is that you or someone you know? Let's be real: We've all experienced trials to varying degrees, but what we do IN those life storms is what makes us into who God wants us to become.

I knew without a doubt God was calling me to write in order to help heal my brokenness—as well as to help others. I was called to share my story, though it is not one I would have chosen if I could have selected it from the shelf in God's library. Still, it is the path God has allowed for me, and He makes no mistakes.

Even before I knew my years of storms were approaching, God was preparing me for them through my grandparents who shared fascinating stories with me almost every time I visited their home. Their successes, struggles, hardships, and hurdles painted pictures that filled my imagination with hope, and yet braced my heart for unwelcome tragedies. Their godly advice was always presented to me like a gift, wrapping me in their love.

Both grew up in the Great Depression and learned how to survive on very little. Their love for the Lord and each other, though, was overflowing. Their stories taught me that trials in life are inevitable no matter how much love is shared between people, within families, and no matter how hard a person works or prepares. Loss of business, loss of loved ones, financial and health struggles: They come a knockin'. While listening to their narratives, I remember believing I could prepare for and possibly prevent future storms.

No one, though, can foretell how hard the winds are going to blow. And yet, it's what we do—and whom we become—during those storms of life that really matter.

I'm ever grateful my parents took me to church, and my grandparents' stories provided a compass that would set me on the right course in troubled times. Sorry, but it hasn't always been pretty. After all, hard times do bring out the best and worst in all of us. Yet, as an adult and growing up in the Christian faith, I trusted this foundation and have discovered God's Word and my Lord Jesus Christ to always have the answers I need.

And now, I have my own stories to tell.

So, my friend, here you are. Since you are reading this book, you may have either gone through a trying time, are going through a life challenge, or know someone who is hurting deeply from a devastating circumstance. Please let me wrap that ribbon of love around you through these pages, and let's learn from the successes and struggles of others. I believe God allows storms in our lives to draw us closer to Him—if we so choose. Let's pause and learn not only from *our* storms but also from others'.

In the midst of the storm, you may be surprised at whom you become, and there are blessings to be found as well. It's time to get up, get going, and be used to your fullest potential for Christ.

I have prayed for you.

Virginia C. Denmark

chapter 1
VISIONARY
OR VICTIM?

NEHEMIAH

Victim:
Someone or something sacrificed or preyed upon

Visionary:
Someone who has clear ideas or hopes of how something
should be done or how things will be in the future

My husband and I worked in the homeless rescue and recovery
ministry collectively for nearly twenty years. We later started our
own business, which we ran for a decade. During that time, the
Lord blessed us in many ways. In turn, we were able to be a
financial blessing to others, to our church, and organizations.
We also saved for retirement, we vacationed, and we had more
than our basic needs met by the Lord. Then, in order to help

my husband's parents—one who had Alzheimer's disease—we decided to move into a larger home and become a blended family.

The year was 2008. We had high hopes for the future, but the economy crashed a few months after we moved into our new home, and our train wreck began approaching fast and furious—with no mercy.

During this period, our family experienced the gripping sadness of loss and death: My father had passed in 2005, but my grandfather, my mother, my father-in-law, and my grandmother all passed within a few years of each other beginning in 2008. We also lost all five of our pets to death. We had to close our business due to unscrupulous corporate representatives and corporate dealings, which also affected others nationwide.

We lost our insurance. Our savings was depleted. Dealing with the losses and challenges that come with Alzheimer's and a blended family were difficult as well. Then in 2011, we had another hard hit: My husband was diagnosed with prostate cancer. By 2012, my daughter's confidence was fading because she was being bullied for the first time in her life. The year 2014 arrived with no good tidings, and things were eventually so bad we lost our home.

Life was a mess.

It was the first time I truly understood what a train wreck life could be. If you watch a train wreck in slow motion, you will witness each car hurtle off the main tracks. You see it coming but can't stop it. You want to shout, "Noooooo!" in hopes of freezing all the chaos before it crashes into a heap of destruction.

But that's not possible. The momentum is already there, and there are sure to be casualties.

As my family pressed through each day, we asked God what He wanted us to do. We were in pain, and no one could help. What was His plan in all of this trouble? Was He disappointed in us? Was it a punishment? What direction did the Lord want us to take? Though my husband and I had applied for work across the country, nothing opened for us. Then, our short-term answer finally came.

God gave us a vision: volunteer more. Now, what kind of vision was that, especially in the midst of all our hardships? We didn't understand, but we acted and served Him through even more volunteer roles.

We were already volunteering at our church, but God wanted us to trust Him and give more of our time. It was clear where God wanted us: our church and our Christian academy. God placed on my heart a vision to start a cheer squad, investing hours in young girls' lives as prayer warriors/cheerleaders, and only God Himself could have done that through me! I taught a Newsletter and Media class and produced a quarterly student newsletter that was printed by a local company. I headed the Float Committee. I learned how to run the commercial kitchen and trained many others.

I was also the PTO (Parent/Teacher Organization) president for several years where we raised money for scholarships, gym flooring, and a gym scoreboard—things that had never been done before. I also enhanced my graphics skills training on new commercial software. My husband volunteered more and more in leadership roles at our church—music, numerous committees—and he eventually became a volunteer associate pastor, utilizing his seminary degree.

During this time, God also opened the doors for us to become employed at the academy; God had moved us back into full-time ministry. It was also when God gave me the vision for this book. I realized He had not allowed all this trouble just for my family's sake, yet it was to grow me in order to be able to help others going through many different life challenges. He had different plans for us, if we were willing to seek His will and trust Him along the way. You see, life is a passage, a journey, a voyage of tears that helps prepare us to be more like Jesus. Hard times are meant to draw one closer to God. The problem is many times people feel like victims and question God's love.

Psalm 55:6 expresses the heartache I felt when everything began collapsing around my family:

> *"And I said, Oh that I had wings like a dove! for then would I fly away, and be at rest."*

Sometimes life was so hard I wanted to disappear! Have you ever felt like that? Well, if life is meant to help us become more like Christ, then how can we see ourselves as victims during hard times? If we turn around that type of thinking, we can look at life through the eyes of someone who can take difficult situations and see the victory at the end: That's a visionary.

There are many people in God's Word who faced their own storms. Nehemiah is someone to be especially admired. He was King Artaxerxes's cup bearer, and his responsibility was to ensure the king's beverages were safe, even to the point that he had to test them himself. It was vital for the king to place someone he trusted in this position and not a potential traitor. Nehemiah was so devoted to his king that he was willing to give his life for him.

Nehemiah loved his fellow Jews, even though he was not living among them. It was within the king's palace that Nehemiah learned the walls of Jerusalem were broken and the gates burned. The Jews in Israel were under constant attack, and Nehemiah was not there to help. What could he do anyway? He was a servant bound to King Artaxerxes's safety. So, Nehemiah turned to the Holy Lord and prayed before Him daily on behalf of his fellow Jews.

It is important to know that Nehemiah mourned, fasted, and lifted up intercessory, confessional prayers before God. (Nehemiah 1:3–7) He knew life was getting more and more troublesome and would soon be devastating if God did not intervene on their behalf.

Nehemiah understood God's chosen people had moved away from God's commandments, and the only way to overcome was through divine forgiveness. What a special man! He was thinking of the welfare of others. Nehemiah's desire to help his people was growing, and deep concern began showing in his countenance.

It's important to note what a great spirit Nehemiah had even as a servant. He was faithful and dependable, as evident in his position. We know he was also a pleasant person because Nehemiah 2:7 states he had never been sad in the king's presence. How many of us can say that about our work days? We can choose where we spend our forty hours earning a living, but Nehemiah didn't even have his freedom.

Concealing his true emotions about his peoples' needs, though, became impossible, and the king took notice. (Nehemiah 2:1–7) Artaxerxes could have responded in several ways: He could have punished Nehemiah; he could have chosen to ignore it, maybe dismissed him, and chosen another cup bearer; or he could have had him put to death. Instead, the king asked him why he was feeling down.

Remember, Nehemiah was prayed up! He was prepared for this moment in his life. His petition was similar to Queen Esther's when *she* was prayed up too and prepared for the most important time in her life! Here's Nehemiah's petition:

> *And I said unto the king, If it please the king and if thy servant have found favour in thy sight, that thou wouldest send me into Judah, unto the city of my fathers' sepulchres, that I may build it.*
> *(Nehemiah 2:5)*

After listening—get that, listening—the king gave Nehemiah permission to leave his position temporarily in order to rebuild in Judah. Nehemiah was given protection and a letter to Asaph who kept the king's forest so he could have the necessary timber. Nehemiah obviously couldn't ride down to the local Lowe's or Home Depot, so God provided ALL he needed to accomplish the job. While others saw the letters of support as coming from King Artaxerxes, Nehemiah knew it was all granted from God. (Nehemiah 2:8)

Nehemiah was in Judah three days before he revealed his true purpose. And here it is: Nehemiah states in 2:11–12 that God placed a VISION in his heart to rebuild the broken wall and gates. His speech motivated and inspired others to work alongside one another building gates and portions of the wall. Some were rebuilding, some were protecting them while they built, and some carried swords while also hauling supplies. It took someone with a willing and praying heart to make this happen.

That's not all! God used Nehemiah for something more.

Ever wonder why the Jews had not already banded together and rebuilt the walls and gate? It's because they saw themselves as *victims*. Even though years earlier Cyrus had given the Jews permission to return to their homeland and rebuild, they couldn't get it done for several reasons. It wasn't until Nehemiah finally came with God's vision that the Jews cried out because of oppression not only from people like Sanballat, Tobiah, and many others, but even from their own brethren. (Nehemiah 5)

There was a famine in the land, and many had sold or mortgaged their properties to have enough food. Some of their children were even now slaves, and they weren't able to redeem them. It's amazing to consider this situation. During a famine, there isn't enough food, so people become weak, depressed, and desperate—even sickly and some die. YET GOD sent a man to give them hope, and GOD gave them the strength to carry heavy supplies to build, fight, and protect themselves all at the same time!

Nehemiah was angry about this oppression because he couldn't understand why even his fellow Jews would put their own people into bondage. He assembled a large group and demanded all be restored, which is what resulted. Can you imagine how that must have felt to everyone?

Nehemiah: Slave. Cup bearer. Visionary. Builder. Protector. Judge. God anointed Nehemiah with all he needed to achieve his God-given vision—even boldness to step forward in the first place.

What would have happened, though, if Nehemiah had seen himself as a victim? Thank God he didn't! He wasn't depressed because he was a servant; he always performed at his best daily. He didn't bury himself in his covers at night in hopes the broken wall and lack of safety for his people would disappear if he closed his eyes. Life wasn't easy; Nehemiah had enemies who worked against him, even though he had the king's permission to rebuild the wall. Nehemiah and his fellow Israelites had to work day and night and also guard while they were rebuilding.

He didn't stay down and depressed because he was not in a position to do anything about a problem. Nehemiah was used by God because of his willingness to *be* used. He had a repentant heart, and through intercessory prayers lifted up God's promise before the Lord to restore His people.

God's plans can be quite surprising.

Furthermore, Nehemiah was confident he would be successful: "Then answered I them, and said unto them, The God of heaven, he will prosper us; therefore we his servants will arise and build: but ye have no portion, nor right, nor memorial, in Jerusalem." (Nehemiah 2:20) He did what he could during troublesome times. He humbled himself before the Lord, prayed, and asked for forgiveness for himself and his nation. He wanted to be a part of God's solution to help others. In doing so, God turned a could-be victim into a visionary and hero who we still talk about today.

TAKEAWAYS

- God will use those who are willing to be used.
- Even when you only see brokenness, God still has a wonderful plan.
- You can expect adversity when you put your hand to God's work.

study questions

What kind of faith did Nehemiah have serving pleasantly daily as the king's cup bearer?

_____

_____

_____

_____

_____

Why was he able to have this kind of faith living as a slave?

_____

_____

_____

_____

_____

_____

When we're doing the Lord's work, we should not be surprised when naysayers and enemies attack. How should we keep moving forward?

_____

_____

_____

_____

_____

_____

Prayer can break through in such miraculous ways so that no matter our position in life, we can do exceedingly more for Christ than our minds can even imagine. What type of person is God looking for to use?

_____

_____

_____

_____

_____

_____

What is a vision for ministry the Lord has placed on your heart, yet you have not acted upon it?

_____

_____

_____

_____

_____

_____

Why not?

_____

_____

_____

_____

_____

_____

What do you need to do to get started?

_____

_____

_____

_____

_____

_____

chapter 2

CRIPPLED OR CROWNED?

MEPHIBOSHETH

> **Crippled:**
> Unable to walk or move properly; disabled
>
> **Crowned:**
> The triumphant culmination of an effort or endeavor,
> especially a prolonged one

If you have experienced the pangs of death of a loved one, you know it can cripple a person emotionally—maybe temporarily—but sometimes grief can cause sickness and even death. I know someone who I believe died of a broken heart after the sudden passing of a loved one. My grandparents also went through something no parent should have to experience: the death of a child. As early as my preteen years, I loved hearing stories of my uncle who passed when I was a toddler. My uncle's eyes were the color of a cloudless, blue sky. His perfect smile in his photographs always left me with the feeling that all good things would come my way. Talk about talent! He played the electric guitar and was a long-distance runner who held a high school record for a while. He had just reassured my grandfather of his salvation when he was married at twenty-one. A short time later, his wedding announcement was featured in the local paper along with his obituary because while working the night shift, he was pulled into a large piece of machinery and was gone with no goodbyes.

Now, that's a storm no one should have to weather. It leaves its mark in a person's soul. Even if you think no one can see, it's there and without warning can bring us low at the whisper of remembrance, for grief speaks all languages.

Storms can make a person bitter or better, sweeter or stagnant. It's a choice, and it can be a hard one to make depending upon your spiritual focus. It wasn't until I grew in maturity and began asking more probing questions when my grandparents shared more of the pain, and even those stories were told in love. After my uncle's death, my grandparents went through the grieving process and had some battles to overcome, but they still chose to focus on the Lord. They always told me they believed the Lord was protecting my uncle from something and took him Home early to Heaven.

My grandparents moved forward making the most of the rest of their lives, holding in their hearts the assurance my uncle had given them only weeks prior: He was with the Lord. In their golden years, they traveled with church friends, taught Sunday school, and led a weekday Bible study group called J.O.Y.: Just Older Youth. They loved that name and what it represented. They brought out all of their homemade teaching tools every time I visited, like the hand-crocheted Betsy Ross and her tiny American flag. My grandfather even preached whenever the opportunity was given him. They were founding members of their beloved church, and people loved my grandparents. I loved them. They exhibited true joy that comes only from faith in our Holy Lord of Comfort. They chose neither to be crippled emotionally nor spiritually by grief. They understood they could move through the storm and focus on Christ's Kingdom with help through a rich, daily prayer life.

But then there are the physical challenges, those that cripple or handicap a person. In the Bible, Mephibosheth comes to mind.

Who is Mephibosheth? I mean, what a name! For starters, he was a king's grandson and was also an heir to the throne. With a grandfather like King Saul—the first king of Israel—he had a lot to live up to. His father was kind-hearted Jonathan, King David's best friend. Mephibosheth had a bright future and the pleasures of life at his fingertips. Any worries in his young life were sure to have been handled in a quick manner.

But that was before a storm blew his way.

In order to really know Mephibosheth's story, let me take you back some years before his birth. The Jews wanted a king like other nations had because Samuel's sons had not followed after God. Without seeking God, they chose Saul to be their king only because of his stature because he was taller than anyone else and made a striking presence. (1 Samuel 9:2) This was not God's perfect will, and He told them through Samuel (the last judge) that Saul would bring hardships, servanthood, and worse. The people chose man over God's leadership at that moment. And God permitted it. Nonetheless, they were warned.

Now, David was God's choice for king and was anointed by Samuel. You remember David: He killed a lion with his bare hands, he killed Goliath the giant with a sling and a smooth stone, and he was a musician and a shepherd. He became a warrior who had to run from King Saul due to a jealous spirit. Saul even attempted to murder him multiple times, but Saul's son Jonathan helped save David's life because they were kindred spirits—rarely seen in one's lifetime. It was this friendship that would last beyond the grave.

Leap ahead to the final battle with the Philistines where Saul, Jonathan, two other sons, his armor bearer, and all of his men lost their lives. (1 Samuel 31) David mourned deeply over their deaths and declared how great both Saul and Jonathan were. (2 Samuel 1) Jonathan and David shared a deep brotherly love for one another—an admiration that surpassed any love for a woman that David had ever experienced in that time in his life. (2 Samuel 1:26) David was deeply devoted to Jonathan for having saved his life.

It was at the announcement of King Saul's death that there was panic back home. Usually when a new king takes over, it could mean the death of rival heirs to the throne, including relatives. The not-so-good news reached Mephibosheth's nursemaid who set herself into panic mode. She scooped up five-year-old Mephibosheth and made a split-second decision that would change his life forever: She turned, ran, and tripped, injuring his feet for life. (2 Samuel 4:4) A terrible accident! Mephibosheth's perfect life as he knew it came to a halt, and he became an orphan and a cripple.

The House of Judah appointed David king, but one of Saul's other sons, Ish-bosheth, was made king over the other eleven tribes. During this time, David increased in popularity and strength so that when Ish-bosheth was eventually killed, David became ruler over Israel.

Here's where we find Mephibosheth as an adult living at the mercy and condescending ridicule of others. How can we know this? Because he thought of himself, "…such a dead dog as I am?" (2 Samuel 9:8) He had no one to encourage him or treat him with respect; therefore, he felt so low as to call himself not even a dog but a dead one. A dead dog can be found lying on the side of a road, cast off as one of the lowest states to consider oneself—one without hope. He also had an unfaithful servant in Ziba. (2 Samuel 16:3) And Mephibosheth lived much of his life in someone else's home in the area called Lodebar, which means "no pasture." So, he grew up believing he was beneath even those who served him before his fall.

Close your eyes and think through these sentences visually. A place where there is no pasture could be brown, barren, fruitless. No one would really want to live in a place like that unless out of necessity for survival. Storms in life can make a person feel deserted, forgotten, unfavored, and maybe even like "…a dead dog."

But God stirred up King David's memory, and he started thinking about Jonathan again.

> *And there was of the house of Saul a servant whose name was Ziba. And when they had called him unto David, the king said unto him, Art thou Ziba? And he said, Thy servant is he. And the king said, Is there not yet any of the house of Saul, that I may shew the kindness of God unto him? And Ziba said unto the king, Jonathan hath yet a son, which is lame on his feet. And the king said unto him, Where is he? And Ziba said unto the king, Behold, he is in the house of Machir, the son of Ammiel, in Lodebar.*
> *(2 Samuel 9:2–4)*

Now, it's hard to determine whether Ziba had good intentions of so freely answering King David. He wasn't a good friend to Mephibosheth, and he proved later he wasn't honest. At that moment, he didn't know whether King David was being forthright about wanting to help a relative of Saul's or Jonathan's.

For all Ziba knew, it could have meant death for Mephibosheth. But at least he answered David honestly.

For Mephibosheth, it must have been a frightening matter to be called upon by the king who was a known enemy of his grandfather's. Still, he went, and that's when he "...bowed himself, and said, 'What is thy servant, that thou shouldest look upon such a dead dog as I am?'" (2 Samuel 9:8)

It's clear what kind of man he was: one with no positive self-esteem because of his crippled feet, his low position in life, loss of his family and inheritance, his reliance upon others for his livelihood, and how others treated him. He exhibited no animosity toward King David, only humility. There was no sign of bitterness in his heart toward anyone. He was his father's son.

What Mephibosheth and others were not aware of though was David and Jonathan's friendship. David wanted to seek out any of Jonathan's relatives so he could shower some kindness upon them for Jonathan's sake. Mephibosheth was brought before David, humbled, and David lifted him up to the position of royalty.

Then the king called to Ziba, Saul's servant, and said unto him, I have given unto thy master's son all that pertained to Saul and to all his house. Thou therefore, and thy sons, and thy servants, shall till the land for him, and thou shalt bring in the fruits, that thy master's son may have food to eat: but Mephibosheth thy master's son shall eat bread alway at my table. Now Ziba had fifteen sons and twenty servants. Then

*said Ziba unto the king, according to all that my
lord the king hath commanded his servant, so shall
thy servant do. As for Mephibosheth, said the king,
he shall eat at my table, as one of the king's sons.*
(2 Samuel 9:9–11)

David lifted up and permitted Mephibosheth to be treated like
royalty, like the son of a king he actually was. He restored all of
King Saul's property to Mephibosheth. The servants, including
Ziba and his sons who probably treated him unkindly, were
commanded to till the fields, take care of their home, and provide
for their needs, and Mephibosheth was allowed to always eat at
King David's table. While it would never be possible for neither
Mephibosheth nor his son to be rulers over Israel—as that was
not God's perfect will—he was certainly treated like crowned
royalty. He had been brought low through a terrible storm in life
that continued for many years, but his heritage was restored by
the grace of God.

There was one glimmer of hope about Mephibosheth, and that
is the fact he had a young son, although there was no mention
of a wife. Somewhere inside of Mephibosheth there must have
been a spark of hope for a happier future, a desire for a family.
Every parent wants a better life for his or her children. I'm sure
Mephibosheth said to himself, "Oh, if only I could get my child
away from this dreary place and these hateful people. If only I
could send him to school and buy new clothes for him, like the
ones I used to wear when I was young. If only he realized he is the
great-grandson of a king!" He also probably didn't want his son
growing up embarrassed of him or wrongfully influenced in life.

I believe he was a praying man with a dream in his heart that seemed unattainable except through God's divine mercy. That mercy manifested itself through King David's kindness divinely ordained by the Lord. We must always trust and believe, even in our most crippling circumstances, that there is always hope through Jesus.

TAKEAWAYS

- Our best is yet to come when we put Christ first.

- There is always hope when we are connected to God.

- God can use others to bless us.

- There is no place too low where God does not know where we are.

- God sees when others misuse us.

study questions

Is there something that has crippled you spiritually that is still preventing you from leading the best life God has for you? If so, what is it and when have you recently lifted it up to the Lord?

_____

_____

_____

_____

_____

_____

What is something that has crippled you emotionally or even physically, hindering you or causing you to feel low?

_____

_____

_____

_____

_____

_____

What different choices can you make about them?

_____

_____

_____

_____

_____

Is there bitterness in your heart toward someone or something that harmed you?

_____

_____

_____

_____

_____

What should you do?

_____

_____

_____

_____

If you said, yes to any of these questions, what steps can you take to draw yourself closer to the Lord, allowing Him to heal, bless, and "crown" you for His perfect will for your life?

_____

_____

_____

_____

_____

_____

chapter 3

WARRIOR
OR WORRIER?

DAVID AND GOLIATH

> **Warrior:**
> A brave or experienced soldier or fighter
>
> **Worrier:**
> Someone who distresses or is troubled

In a safe place in my home is a keepsake I won in fifth grade. That year, Coach Groves coordinated a Mini-Olympics competition. At the end of the games, I was standing center, presented with the top award for girls: a gold-painted, hand-cut, wooden medallion I wore the remainder of the day. It was beautiful, and I believed even the authentic Olympic gold medal could be no more special than the one that adorned my neck with gold and red twine.

What I didn't know at that young age was that I accomplished more than simply winning a top prize out of two classes of ten-year-old girls. I recall looking down at the medal on my way to lunch and marching headfirst into my dad's chest; somehow he learned of my win, drove to my school, and wrapped his strong arms around me. He was so proud. Later that day, my mother, siblings, and I turned into our driveway. The pine trees that lined the road all seemed to wait in anticipation, slowly revealing what could be seen as we rounded the corner and were greeted with a "Welcome Home, Champ!" banner Dad had made and hung on the garage door.

My dad thought I was a champ.

I've kept the "The Gold" for nostalgic purposes, and as I reminisce, it amazes me that at that young age I knew I needed to keep my wits about me to be a winner. I had to remain positive and focused through each stage of the multievent competition. I had to be bold and fearless for the prize. I remember telling myself I could outrun all of the girls. I knew my strengths and weaknesses and believed that gold prize was mine.

Ah, youth. Sometimes I think I had more courage when I was younger simply because I didn't see all the dangers life presented. Like, "What if this happens...or that?" Oh, my word! Would I have ever stepped into the imaginary Olympic wrestling box and faced my opponent—including the toughest girl my age—if I allowed those questions to blind me of my potential? I doubt it.

Worrying opens the door for fear, which ultimately kicks back and settles in the heart. It's why our hearts get sick at times, not allowing us to move forward to reach our full potential for Christ.

God's Word states He has given us power, love, and a sound mind. (2 Timothy 1:7) We are NOT to be worriers but warriors pressing for that prize of God's high calling upon our lives. (Philippians 3:14)

Who knew an elementary school student could be a champion? Well, in the eyes of my family I was.

In the Bible, there is a much-told story of a champion from the city of Gath. (1 Samuel 17:4) The Bible is very clear giants existed. Gath, one of the great five Philistine cities, was only one of many places all over the world where giants have been sighted—and their skeletons unearthed.

We don't really know how old he was, but we do know this champion was a grown man who had been a warrior since his youth. (1 Samuel 17:33) His story has become legend through a final battle with a younger warrior. This champion fought in the Philistine army and was known for his conquests, abilities, fearlessness, and height. You see, he was the infamous giant named Goliath. He stood more than nine feet tall and had the strength to match his stature.

His ego was even bigger. Oh, it's not that he couldn't back it up; I mean, that may have been why the famous phrase, "It ain't braggin' if it's true!" was coined. He had earned the respect of his fellow warriors and those in other lands, even from across the seas where they were known as Caphtorim before being called Philistines.

On one particular day, Goliath found himself impatient and disgusted as he and his fellow Philistines had been camped against King Saul's army on one side of a mountain. Only the Valley of Elah separated them physically; they were close enough to where they could shout and hear one another. They could probably hear the clanging of armor, the restlessness moving about inside the camps, and maybe the sounds of evening laughter as it traveled across the valley.

Goliath considered neither himself nor his fellow Philistines as servants like he saw the Israelites. (1 Samuel 17:8) The Philistine warriors were there at their own choosing, while the Israelites were there under King Saul's leadership. (Remember in chapter 2 where Samuel warned the Jews about getting a king like other nations? They were warned about the consequences, but they paid no attention and left God.) Goliath wasn't the leader of the Philistine's army, as stated in 1 Samuel 17:4–11 where he came "...out of the camp of the Philistines...," and it presented a challenge to the Israelites. This is very telling because no one in the army tried to stop him. Goliath was placing everyone's freedom on the line based on his personal strength. Did no one even look for that nine-foot ladder so he could have a personal one-on-one with Goliath? Like, say, climb a few rungs, tap him on his shoulder, and ask, "Uh, whatta ya think you're doing?" No! Not one of the Philistines asked him what he was doing or even attempted to stop him because they believed, based on his track record, that Goliath could stand on his own and come out the champion.

> *And he stood and cried unto the armies of Israel, and said unto them, Why are ye come out to set your battle in array [impressive display]? am not I a Philistine, and ye servants to Saul? choose you a man for you, and let him come down to me. If he be able to fight with me, and to kill me, then will we be your servants; but if I prevail against him, and kill him, then shall ye be our servants, and serve us. And the Philistine said, I defy the armies of Israel this day; give me a man that we may fight together.*
> *(1 Samuel 17:8–10, emphasis added)*

Goliath presented the opportunity to base the entire battle singularly upon one-on-one combat between him and one Jewish warrior. A simple plan.

Well, not so much.

Goliath was imposing, and his challenge left the Jewish army terrified. Even King Saul was too afraid to think straight. Standing over across the valley, the Israelites knew Goliath was a fierce warrior. Imagine the sun reflecting off all that brass covering his nine-foot, six-inch frame and the large shield carried by his personal armor bearer. I can imagine they had to cover their eyes from it during the day. They could probably even feel the echoes of his threatening taunts resounding through the mountains.

It was not much of a surprise when no one stepped up to fight the champion Goliath, so both armies fought down in the Valley of Elah (1 Samuel 17:19), and the battle continued forty days.

Enter young David, recently anointed king of Israel by Samuel, and the youngest of Jesse's eight sons. He had heard King Saul's appeal for soldiers, but only David's three oldest brothers followed into battle. David was only a youth at the time—possibly a preteen—and he returned to feed his father's sheep.

After forty days, Jesse told David to go check on his brothers. He took ten loaves of bread, a bushel of parched corn, and ten cheeses for his brothers' army captain. (1 Samuel 17:17–18) When he arrived, he got out of his carriage and bravely walked right into the middle of the army lining up in the trench. It was morning and time for Goliath to make his sales pitch again—a clear defiance against the army of God's choosing and a fight to the death.

The men took one look at Goliath and started running.

David was in amazement when the soldiers told him all the prizes that would come to the man who would kill Goliath: King Saul would grant him great riches, give his daughter to wed, and free everyone in his father's house. (1 Samuel 17:25) (This was definitely better than ever winning the Publisher's Clearing House Sweepstakes!) Remember, they gave up their freedom when they chose Saul over God.

I can imagine David, who had killed a lion and a bear while protecting his father's sheep, getting into the hype of the winnings, the excitement of the thought of beating the giant… but then his brothers showed up. Now, the older brothers had probably heard that story about the bear and the lion more times than they wanted to hear. Samuel had passed over all of the brothers before anointing David as God's choice for king. Perhaps they saw him as somewhat braggadocious and prideful, but I would also like to think they felt a little protective of him as well.

He was the youngest child. The brothers reprimanded and belittled him (1 Samuel 17:28), asking where were his "few sheep" as if he couldn't even handle those, so how could he even think of joining the ranks? David replied like this: "What have I now done?" (1 Samuel 17:29) That makes me giggle at the thought of the possible back story because it reminds me of Joseph. (That's a story for another day.) We know David was *not* bragging, because in 1 Samuel 17:45–47, he clearly included everyone as having part of the conquer, not just himself.

David turned, listened more to all the other men, and started saying something like, "Who is this man who has defied God's army? Who does he think he is? I have done…" The men got so excited that someone, even a young boy, would express boldness about accepting the challenge, and word traveled quickly to King Saul. This is proof even King Saul was not thinking clearly because he got excited about it too!

Let's pause here and envision how imposing Goliath was in appearance and put it in perspective: At nine foot six, a six-foot-tall man in comparison would have come up somewhere around Goliath's hips or his lower rib cage. Look around your room right now and try to determine the height of your ceiling. Now, keep in mind that giants' skeletons have been found throughout the world reaching extraordinary heights. The height is important because the Jews were terrified, so this indicates that fear of Goliath represented how big their storm was each day; it was enough to send grown warriors running, preventing them from having a clear mind to outsmart or pray for their breakthrough.

King Saul took David aside and acknowledged he was too small for the deed, so he offered his personal armor for the battle. After David put on the armor, he said he couldn't use them because he had not "proved them." (1 Samuel 17:39)

> *David said moreover, The Lord that delivered me out*
> *of the paw of the lion, and out of the paw of the bear, he*
> *will deliver me out of the hand of this Philistine. And*
> *Saul said unto David, Go, and the Lord be with thee.*
> *(1 Samuel 17:37)*

Here was a king, chosen by the nation of Israel, who was neither as brave nor prepared for battle as young David. I mean, Saul was thrilled to finally have anyone willing to fight Goliath. He set David on his way, probably with a pat on his back while saying, "Go ahead. I'll be here at the camp waiting on you, [then under his breath] 'cause I'm sho' 'nuff not gonna go with you."

David met Goliath with his staff, five smooth stones from the nearest brook, and his sling. Goliath was mortified and insulted that the Jewish army would send a *boy* to fight him. He said, "Am I a dog that thou comest to me with staves? And the Philistine cursed David by his gods." (1 Samuel 17:43) Oh, what a show that must have been with Goliath's powerful anger on display! It was probably a fanfare of a fit.

And here is the defining difference between these two warriors: Goliath recognized his gods and David recognized he would win, "…but I come to thee in the name of the Lord of hosts, the God of the armies of Israel, whom thou has defied." (1 Samuel 17:45) Even King Saul recognized in verse 37 that it would take God's blessing to win against the giant.

> *Then said David to the Philistine, Thou comest to me with a sword, and with a spear, and with a shield: but I come to thee in the name of the Lord of hosts, the God of the armies of Israel, whom thou hast defied. This day will the Lord deliver thee into mine hand; and I will smite thee, and take thine head from thee; and I will give the carcasses of the host of the Philistines this day unto the fowls of the air, and to the wild beasts of the earth; that all the earth may know that there is a God in Israel. And all this assembly shall know that the Lord saveth not with sword and spear: for the battle is the Lord's, and he will give you into our hands.*
> *(1 Samuel 17:45–47)*

Down went Goliath. Off went his head. Away went the Philistine army as they fled for their lives. Up went the shouts of the Israelites as they pursued their enemies and conquered them. After forty days of battle, young David did what an entire army of skilled yet worried soldiers could not. He faced a battle, acknowledged God as the reason for previous victories in his life, and was assured God would overcome this newest battle as well.

David: A young shepherd boy running errands for his father who became renown for saving Israel one morning with the anointing of God. He was a warrior in faith and became a nation's champion that day. God was pleased and considered him a champion even when no one else did.

TAKEAWAYS

- David didn't pray for God to take away Goliath. He used past successes to remind himself of how God prevailed in his life and went forward in the name of the Lord. We can be godly warriors during our storms when we remember our previous triumphs through Christ and move forward in faith.

- The Israeli army continued fighting the Philistines during those forty days, so it can be said it was easier for the soldiers to fight the battle together. This should be an example of our prayer lives when we need others to pray for us while in a terrible storm. Sometimes we feel we just can't handle the storms alone. It was easier for them to come together and fight as one than to send ONE MAN to fight Goliath. Why? Because no one was prepared to handle that storm on their own, until young David stepped into the trench and remembered what God had already done for him and through him.

- Faith trumps fanfare: The battle is the Lord's.

study questions

Who were the worriers in this story?

_____

_____

_____

_____

_____

_____

Did the Jewish army believe God was on their side? Why?

_____

_____

_____

_____

_____

What do you think the life of a shepherd was like for David?

_____

_____

In addition to killing the lion and the bear, what do you think
helped strengthen David's faith?

The soldiers left their families behind and knew their failure
would result in enslavement or death, so what do you think was
going through their minds while they went into battle? (See 1
Samuel 17:19.)

Has there been a time in your life when you felt more like a worrier than a warrior? What changed your heart and mindset at that time?

_____

_____

_____

_____

_____

How can you apply this story in the midst of your hardships to remind yourself we are warriors in faith? List some times when your faith prevailed and God answered your prayers in a remarkable way.

_____

_____

_____

_____

_____

chapter 4
[SELF-] RIGHTEOUS OR REDIRECTED?

P A U L / S A U L

> **Righteous:**
> Morally right, justifiable in one's mind
>
> **Redirected:**
> Direct something to a new or different place or purpose

In the introduction to this book, I mentioned the tornado that touched down and destroyed almost all of the trees in my yard, including many that were adjacent to my property. That was February 2017. I felt excited knowing the evil one was mad about the book and the Bible study—both of which manifested out of so much pain. As if throwing a tantrum, the angry winds blew in and uprooted our magnificent old oaks, splintered almost all of the other trees in our yard, and yet my family was safe and our home remained intact.

The roof, though, would require repair.

After a while, we finally decided on a roofer and set in motion the plan to make the repairs. One late afternoon after work, I heard heavy steps and pounding on my rooftop. Assuming it was the roofer, I walked outside to speak with him and his crew, but all I saw was a work truck parked in front of my home. I knew he was busy, so I left him to his work. About fifteen minutes passed before the noises stopped, and I saw two men standing on my back deck. With arms crossed, they appeared puzzled and deep in thought. I didn't recognize them and started watching their next movements. They were eyeing my dining room bay window and proceeded to measure it, and then took a few steps back to look at it again.

At that point, I pulled out my cell phone and snapped a few pictures, which I promptly sent to my husband with the caption, "Who are these men?"

Without waiting for a reply, I opened my back door, stepped outside, smiled, and said, "Excuse me. I don't believe I know you men."

The elder of the two men quipped back, "I don't know you either!" and snickered while looking at his coworker.

I responded, "Yes, but you are on *my* property."

You can imagine their blank, wide-eyed expressions as they stammered to respond, all while my protective black lab was at my side barking at them. They finally told me to speak with the third member of the crew who was rounding the corner of my home. Convenient.

Very calmly, questions began again. Still, I was confused, and they were confused. I didn't give them any insight because I was expecting *them* to give answer as to why they were measuring my roof, bay window, and were on my property in general. For a few moments, it seemed they were trying to convince me *they* were in the right! I mean, it was obvious I needed roof repair (to say the least), but it took getting down to the actual work site address before we reached the "Ah, ha" moment: They were supposed to be working on the house next door.

They said, "Oh, we were wondering how we were going to put a French door in the bay window!"

Can you imagine what would have happened if I had not been home? These were professional roofers. They were licensed. They had the right tools in hand and were equipped for the task. They had been recommended for hire. They were intent on accomplishing an excellent repair job. The problem? They were on the wrong roof. The wrong property. The wrong path in general. Even the series of questions didn't seem to convince them there was a problem until the truth lay present and obvious. Disaster was avoided only after I intervened to stop them in their tracks and redirected them. I bet they never make that mistake again.

Now, before we get all up in a team chant about how bad that mistake was, let's remember we are all human. We've all made mistakes. Thankfully, mistakes may be discovered in private, and we don't have to cut and run or face the music, as the sayings go.

I will say the roofers handled themselves very well with the news of their mistake. They apologized and quickly relocated their business next door—probably grateful to have been spared the costly disaster.

I thought about that situation for a week and knew there was more than one lesson in it. What was the Lord trying to show me? I asked Him numerous times, but the answer evaded me until one Sunday night following church; during some quiet time with God, He reminded me of the story of a tentmaker traveling boldly down a road on a mission, until a storm swept in and redirected his life.

This was no average trip for this tentmaker. He was a diligent man, pious and passionate about his religion, even to the imprisonment and death of many who did not hold to his same beliefs—namely Christians. You see, this traveler was a Roman Pharisee, and his name was Saul.

Saul's age at that time is not known to us, but we do know he was young when another young man named Stephen was martyred for his Christian testimony. (Acts 7:54–60) Scripture doesn't state Saul was among those who stoned Stephen, but he was standing close enough for the witnesses to lay—not toss or throw—their clothes down at his feet during those horrible moments. The crowd wanted no constraints from their clothing, or maybe they didn't want to get their coats dirty while they took the life of an innocent man who was sold-out for Christ.

Saul knew what was happening and didn't make a run for it. He stayed. He watched. He relished in the moment and was inspired. Make no mistake: Saul was an active participant by "guarding" the clothes the murderers had placed at his feet while the sweet spirit of Stephen left this earth and was received by Jesus.

Saul also joined in the yelling, encouraging the stone-throwing commotion conducted on the outskirts of the city as indicated in Acts 8:1, which states Saul was "consenting unto his [Stephen's] death."

Guilty.

Was this Saul's first time being party to a stoning of a Christian? Not sure, but since he was young and not actually throwing the stones, one may surmise it was among his first. It didn't take long for his zeal against Christians to grow. Acts 9:1 states he was exceptionally vocal against Christians by this time, to the point of making death threats. It actually states he was "breathing out" the threats, so it was constantly on his mind and his tongue. He was probably obsessed with the idea of obliterating the saints because he believed it was the right thing to do.

Jesus had much criticism for the Pharisees who lived an outwardly righteous lifestyle. They were into ceremonies and rigidness and not matters of true spiritual redemption. They were self-righteous.

In fact, the Pharisees were the religious sect that plotted the death of Jesus Christ.

By the time Saul was becoming bolder about his religious convictions, he was also becoming well-known—maybe infamous—in Jerusalem and beyond for his evil acts against Christians. (Acts 9:13) People were talking about Saul, and we know bad news always travels faster and farther than any positive news does. In order to make good on his threats, Saul even requested permission of the high priest so he could travel to Damascus and bring back any man or woman who proclaimed the name of Jesus Christ. (Acts 9:2) He was obsessed. Possessed. Just what would the Pharisaical leadership think of him when he returned to Jerusalem with more Christians bound and set for termination?

He and his travel "crew" packed their bags, their supplies, the high priest's letters of authority, and set forth on the road to Damascus heading straight into an impending storm. Much like the roofers earlier in this chapter, Saul and his crew were licensed. They had the right tools in hand and were equipped for the task. They were intent on accomplishing an excellent job, and they set out to get it done.

Today, a trip over land from Jerusalem to Damascus would require at least 400 miles of travel distance round trip. Saul's journey was going to take many weeks, maybe a couple of months, for him to arrive in Damascus. But he wouldn't arrive without reputation because the people of Damascus had already heard of Saul. And it wasn't good.

Saul pressed on anxious to arrive in Damascus to present his letters of authority. He had traveled a long time and was almost at his destination when something incredible happened. Unexpectedly. With a force so bright it sent Saul trembling to the ground.

A light! From Heaven! One moment, Saul and his team were walking along or riding...and *bam!* He was hit with a light so brilliant that it shocked Saul right to the ground! His face was probably pressed in the dirt, eyes closed, with his hands and arms covering his head. What in the world?

Well, it wasn't of *this* world: It was Jesus stopping Saul right in his tracks.

> *And he fell to the earth, and heard a voice saying unto him, Saul, Saul, why persecutest thou me? And he said, Who art thou, Lord? And the Lord said, I am Jesus whom thou persecutest: it is hard for thee to kick against the pricks. And he trembling and astonished said, Lord, what wilt though have me to do? And the Lord said unto him, Arise, and go into the city, and it shall be told thee what thou must do.*
> *(Acts 9:4–6)*

Now, isn't it just like human nature to fall to our knees in a time of crisis? It's important to note that Saul, who never acknowledged the Lord Jesus Christ, immediately addressed the light as "Lord." Not little "l" lord but Lord. Holy God. Sovereign. The One and Only. Jesus presented Himself to Saul and audibly spoke to him. He questioned Saul. He answered Saul and told him who He is.

Now, interesting enough, Saul's "crew" had a different experience.

> *And the men which journeyed with him stood speechless, hearing a voice, but seeing no man.*
> *(Acts 9:7)*

They stood frozen, listening to a Voice they didn't recognize, while Saul was having a discussion with the Lord. Just like the roofing crew in the earlier story, it took the roofer in charge to "see the light" and understand what was really happening in middle of the crisis. It was not until he came in contact with the homeowner that the error was revealed, and at that moment, they all backed down in humility. Something similar happened to Saul. Where was his audacious boldness? He wilted at the first sight of what Jesus allowed him to see of His presence. His Holy Light. It illuminated all around Saul. And this is what the Light of Jesus does: It shines a light on our sins. Once Jesus reveals our sins to us, it's decision time.

What we do at that point is up to us. Saul had asked God what He would have him to do. (Wise decision, Saul.) It was then that Jesus directed Saul to continue into Damascus and then, and only then, would Saul be instructed on what Jesus would have him to do.

When Jesus was finished speaking, the Light disappeared. Then moving with hesitation, Saul stood, lowered his arms, and opened his eyes, only to discover he was blind. Once spiritually blinded by sin, he was now physically blinded by the Light of Truth. What would Saul's next move be?

And Saul arose from the earth; and when his eyes were
opened, he saw no man: but they [his crew] led him by
the hand, and brought him into Damascus. And he was
three days without sight, and neither did eat nor drink.
(Acts 9:8–9, emphasis added)

Here was a religious person doing what he fervently believed was right. Guess what though? There are many people living with a head knowledge of Christ but lacking a true heart relationship with Him. I know a man who had been living a religious Christian lifestyle for years. He was a deacon, a Sunday school teacher, he sang in the church choir, and he helped in the bus ministry. He was very impressive if you were to check off a list of church leadership volunteer roles. He was busy about the Lord's business.

One day, though, God revealed to him in a revival service that he was lost. The spiritual realization of his lost state without Christ put him into a few days of torment where he lost five pounds before giving his life completely over to the Lord. This man is my husband.

I believe this is what happened to Saul. He couldn't eat. He couldn't even drink, which is essential for life. He was under so much conviction that all he could do was pray. He could have continued on his original mission—though blinded—and become even more fervent in his quest. He could have become angry about being blind. He could have become afraid and returned to his home in Jerusalem. He could have given in to the fear of God and hidden himself the rest of his days without being used of Christ. Instead, Saul obeyed Jesus.

Once in Damascus, Saul was guided to the house of a man named Judas (not Iscariot). Saul's life had been turned upside down because he realized everything he had been taught and believed in was a lie. Jesus IS the Messiah. Jesus really IS the Lord of lords the Jews had been waiting for all those years. Now, all he could do was pray (Acts 9:11) until the Lord told him his next steps. It's all he *wanted* to do.

Damascus was a busy city, and somewhere among the many people lived a Christian man named Ananias. As he was resting one day, the Lord spoke to him in a vision and instructed him to visit Saul. But there was the matter of that reputation Saul had built, and Ananias brought this to God's attention (as if God didn't know about it already).

> *Then Ananias answered, Lord, I have heard by many of this man, how much evil he hath done to thy saints at Jerusalem: And here he hath authority from the chief priests to bind all that call on thy name. But the Lord said unto him, Go thy way: for he is a chosen vessel unto me, to bear my name before the Gentiles, and kings, and the children of Israel: For I will shew him how great things he must suffer for my name's sake.*
> *(Acts 9:13–16)*

I'm not sure how much attention Ananias has ever received for his faith action, but he was the one God used to redirect Saul's life. It was that, "Okay, God. Whatever you say!" moment that sent Ananias out of the safety of his home seeking a blind man who was praying desperately to hear again from God.

> *And Ananias went his way and entered into the house; and putting his hands on him said, Brother Saul, the Lord, even Jesus that appeared unto thee in the way as thou camest, hath sent me, that thou mightest receive thy sight, and be filled with the Holy Ghost. And immediately there fell from his eyes as it had been scales: and he received sight forthwith, and arose, and was baptized.*
> *(Acts 9:17–18)*

Immediately following Saul's receiving of the Holy Ghost, he was nourished with food, and then he spent a number of days with the disciples of Christ in Damascus who taught him about Jesus. He was so eager to learn and be used that "straightway he preached Christ" even in the synagogues. (Acts 9:20) What bravery! What boldness for Jesus! He was a changed man and wanted everyone to know it.

It's important to emphasize that Saul immediately knew his purpose in life after being confronted with this life-changing trial: to boldly tell others about Christ and what Jesus did for him on the road to Damascus.

Saul went on to say:

For though I be free from all men, yet have I made
myself servant unto all, that I might gain the more…
To the weak became I as weak, that I might gain the
weak: I am made all things to all men, that I might by
all means save some.
(1 Corinthians 9:19, 22)

After Saul's conversion, he began using his Roman name, Paul, which would be received better by Gentiles than if he used his Jewish name. He was confronted by Jesus. He trusted Jesus and was redirected in his life's purpose. Even though he had been told by Ananias that he would suffer greatly for Christ, which he did, Paul still preached the Gospel and is known as one of the apostles who led many to Christ.

TAKEAWAYS

- We can be righteous and yet still be wrong when we are outside of the will of God.
- While we may start out on the wrong path, God is STILL able to redirect us for His glory.
- Once we have had a true experience with God, we will never be the same person.

study questions

Who do you think could have possibly been some of Saul's/Paul's first Christian converts?

_____

_____

_____

_____

_____

_____

Why?

_____

_____

_____

_____

Why do you think the men in the "crew" could not see the Light or understand the Voice?

_____

_____

_____

_____

_____

_____

Is there some area in your life God wants to redirect? What might it be?

_____

_____

_____

_____

_____

What do you think would have happened to Saul if he had continued on his original quest/path?

_____

_____

_____

_____

_____

chapter 5
COMFORTER OR COMPLAINER?

N A O M I

> **Comforter:**
> One who soothes in time of affliction or distress
>
> **Complainer:**
> A person given to excessive complaints and crying and whining

Something I will always remember is walking through the doors of the ICU and seeing my grandfather's face light up each time I visited. His love for me was evident because he wanted to shield me from his true physical pain. He wanted to place his attention elsewhere, so what did he do? He reached out with a smile on his face and asked how my family and I were doing. He didn't complain about his circumstances and health; he wanted to be a blessing to me. He always was.

My grandfather's demeanor was like this whether he was at home, at church, or at death's door. His life had not been easy, but he always found comfort in the Lord. He was the most patient person I have ever known. He lived a humble life, yet he was a jewel of a man. My son shared a special bond with my grandfather who always encouraged him to obey and to do his best. One day while looking at a photograph of my grandfather when he was young in the service, I noticed his smile was similar to my son's—a hint of bashfulness tucked away in the slightly right-tilted grin. I'm so grateful for those few years when my grandfather offered words of wisdom and direction to me and my children.

Life ought to be like that. As we become more spiritually mature, we should be able to give of ourselves, mentor others, and help guide them on the right path in life. Hardships, though, can do strange things to people.

Take Naomi for example. Her story is told in the book of Ruth, but I think hidden in the passages is a back story with purpose: An unpenned message of faith that was forgotten and ultimately refreshed. This is the history of how one of Naomi's daughters-in-law chose to follow after the Lord, but behind the words is a deeper story that can only be revealed if you look for the heartbeat behind the headliner.

Many people know the wonderful story about Ruth's choice and her ultimate blessing of being in the lineage of our Lord Jesus

Christ. It is *not* well known, though, that the famous phrase displayed in many Christian homes and also promised with devout love in wedding vows was spoken by Ruth to Naomi:

> *...for whither thou goest, I will go; and where thou lodgest, I will lodge: thy people shall be my people, and thy God my God.*
> *(Ruth 1:16)*

Ruth's story is powerful and woven in the hard path Naomi had to take. Let's focus on Naomi, though, whom I believe has been somewhat misunderstood and even overly judged. Remember, it's easy to say what you think *you* would do until you walk through that storm yourself. None of us is perfect, right?

Who was Naomi?

Naomi lived in Bethlehem with her husband, Elimelech, and their two sons during the time of the judges. (Ruth 1) This was before the nation sinned and appointed Saul as king. There was a season of famine in the land, so people were finding it difficult to provide for their families. Elimelech could have stayed and trusted God through his storm, but he made a desperate decision that mirrored the faith level of many yesteryear and today: He moved.

It's also important to understand that when they moved, the family left their homeland, their extended families, their friends, their faith support, and the land where God wanted them to be. They left in hopes of finding a better life in the city of Moab. Elimelech placed his hopes and his family's future in a land of pagans.

The life of a Jewish wife was one of submission and honor to her husband, so when Elimelech decided to move his family, Naomi went, even if she didn't want to go, had doubts about the relocation, and thought his decision was wrong. Did she question Elimelech's decision? Did she inquire whether he sought God, or the elders, on the matter? We don't know.

Another problem with the relocation is where they traveled to live: Moab, a heathen, pagan nation that practiced polygamy, sexual deviations, and idol worship. In fact, Moab's beginnings came from an incestuous relationship. After Lot's escape from Sodom and Gomorrah, he and his daughters fled to Zoar but ultimately moved to a cave in the mountains for safety (which he should have done in the first place at the instruction of the angels). Lot's older daughter conspired with her younger sister to get Lot drunk so they could have children (Lot's seed). There is much that could be said about this because it shows no faith in God for His provision, it demonstrates a lack of respect for their father, and it indicates what kind of environment they had been living in to even consider this deed. Sodom and Gomorrah were so wretched that God destroyed them with brimstone and fire. (Remember Lot's wife? She turned into a pillar of salt for looking back at the destruction.)

Lot's older daughter's son became Father of the Moabites, and the younger daughter's son, Benammi, is Father of the Ammonites who would war with Israel in the future. Think about it: They were all relatives. (Genesis 19)

Return to the future, now, with Elimelech telling Ruth and their two sons that they would be moving to the country of Moab. (Ruth 1:1–2) Their current situation must have been terribly bleak to even consider moving to a pagan land, but that's what they did. Naomi must have known of the possibility that her two sons would take wives from Moab. It makes one wonder if her heart ached over the possibility. Maybe this is where Naomi's heart began despairing because Moabite daughters-in-law would not be of their faith. She may have wondered if they would even get along, show her respect, or turn her sons from their faith.

One may imagine a layer of despair began to reveal itself in Naomi's lowered shoulders as they entered Moab.

What were Elimelech's hopes? To provide for his family? Did he really believe God would honor this move? Had God told him to move? It wasn't long before Elimelech died, leaving behind his wife and two sons whom he led to a pagan land.

At that point, Naomi had lost all glimmer of hope in this land because her husband, the provider and leader, was gone. One may think, *Why didn't she have hope in her sons?* That's a good question that must be explored. The Bible doesn't reveal much about Mahlon and Chilion, but their names do. Even today, many parents choose the names of their children to reflect their hopes or to honor loved ones. In this case, the son's names revealed their health. In Hebrew, Mahlon means "sickly," and Chilion means "pining or wasting away." It's possible the famine caused the sons to be weak and sickly, but that point is not clear. What *is* clear is that the Bible states Mahlon married Ruth, and Chilion married

Orpah, both Moabite women. After about ten years, both of the men died, leaving behind no children, again possibly a reference to their lack of good health. (Ruth 1:4–5)

At this point, Naomi's husband and her two adult sons are gone, leaving her with an uncertain future for her and her daughters-in-law.

Exhale deeply here. There's more.

Naomi's despair had probably turned into a depressive state because she was alone in a foreign country with two daughters-in-law who were not of the Jewish faith. She had no one to provide for them, and a prosperous future seemed unattainable.

She had heard, though, that God had lifted the famine in her home country, so she decided to return. There is something to be said about this decision because it took a trace of bravery, a glint of hope, to even have the energy to move forward and go home. If you have ever experienced the loss of a loved one, your livelihood, and your home, you fully understand how you can experience an in-the-bed, pull-the-covers-over-your-head energy level. In other words, not much is happening. Naomi wanted to return to her homeland and had to put action to the little bit of hope that had surfaced in her heart.

Something else to consider is her relationship with her daughters-in-law. Even during Naomi's loss of her husband and being in a foreign land, she still made a positive impression in the lives of Ruth and Orpah. She must have made both of them feel very welcome and loved in her home. They could have gone on walks and shopped in town together. Maybe they laughed and sang while they cooked and cleaned. Her loving hands showed her daughters-in-law how to care for their sickly husbands—her sons. In the evening, she probably shared stories of her life in Judah. Whatever Naomi did, she won over the hearts of Ruth and Orpah.

To go deeper into Naomi's personality and character, it is highly probable she was a go-getter, someone who could press through hard times and life's storms with a positive mindset. She did, after all, make it through the previous decade-plus years without being known as a complainer. In fact, her very name in Hebrew means "pleasantness," so that is what people thought of Naomi. It's clear she made a positive impression on Orpah and Ruth because they wanted to go with her when she told them she would return to the land of Judah. They rose, probably early morning, and even started on the journey with her. (Ruth 1:7)

The storm, though, had been too long and hard for Naomi. It had beaten against her positive spirit and taken her low. It could happen to anyone, but the real problem lay in the fact that Naomi believed God had dealt bitterly with her. (Ruth 1:20) Maybe she felt she was being punished by God when in fact she and her family were the ones who had left God's perfect will for their lives. She was suffering the consequences of bad decisions.

Naomi had nothing to offer her daughters-in-law but the advice to turn around and go back to their families. Most people think only Ruth wanted to follow Naomi. The truth is, neither of them wanted to return to their homes to start life over with new husbands, but Naomi insisted they return:

> *Turn again, my daughters, go your way; for I am too old to have a husband. If I should say, I have hope, if I should have a husband also to night, and should also bear sons; Would ye tarry for them till they were grown? would ye stay for them from having husbands? nay, my daughters; for it grieveth me much for your sakes that the hand of the Lord is gone out against me.*
> *(Ruth 1:12–13)*

Naomi was sharing all the realistic, negative aspects of where she was in life: no children nor any hope of having more children, which was considered almost like a curse. She was homeless and a widow. Yet, still she laced her comments with hope and some comfort for Ruth and Orpah.

Orpah and Ruth cried and pleaded, and ultimately Orpah took Naomi's sad advice. Why sad? Because Naomi was too depressed to give sound, godly advice. She knew she was sending Orpah back to a heathen nation of Moab, while Judah was God's nation and their only hope. Naomi could not see any hope in *herself* because that was her focus, not God. Though terribly sad to leave Naomi, Orpah decided to follow her mother-in-law's instruction and was never mentioned again in the Bible. It was, after all, her choice to make. Our words of advice are so important and must be bathed in prayer.

Naomi believed God had turned His back on her and believed she was too old to start over in life, yet Ruth loved Naomi so much she pledged to stay with her. (Ruth 1:18)

> *And Ruth said, Entreat me not to leave thee, or to return*
> *from following after thee: for whither thou goest, I will*
> *go; and where thou lodgest, I will lodge: thy people shall*
> *be my people, and thy God my God: Where thou diest,*
> *will I die, and there will I be buried: the Lord do so to*
> *me, and more also, if ought but death part thee and me.*
> *(Ruth 1:16–17)*

Who could say no to that? Naomi couldn't, so she and Ruth journeyed back to Bethlehem together.

Naomi's hardships took a toll on her body and demeanor, so much so that people didn't recognize her when she returned to her homeland. She was probably thin, stooped with hunched shoulders. Her hair had probably turned gray and had thinned. Maybe her clothes were worn, and she no longer cared about her appearance. Perhaps she didn't have a pleasant attitude anymore and had become a complainer. We know this because she wanted to be called "bitter" in order to represent what she knew she had become. She knew it!

When we become bitter we complain. Four times in one scripture Naomi complained that her hardships were God's doings:

> *...Call me not Naomi, call me Mara [bitter]: for the*
> *Almighty hath dealt very bitterly with me. I went out*

full and the Lord hath brought me home again empty:
why then call ye me Naomi, seeing the Lord hath
testified against me, and the Almighty hath afflicted me?
(Ruth 1:20–21, emphasis added)

Bless. Her. Heart. If we all get real with ourselves and God, many of us would say, "I've been there too." When going through a life storm, it's important to surround yourself with loved ones, to have proper nutrition and rest, to have a safe place—a sanctuary—to live, and to have hope. Remember what the Bible states:

Hope deferred maketh the heart sick: but when the
desire cometh, it is a tree of life.
(Proverbs 13:12)

Further consideration comes from instruction out of James:

Let no man say when he is tempted, I am tempted of
God; for God cannot be tempted with evil, neither
tempteth he any man: but every man is tempted,
when he is drawn away of his own lust, and enticed.
Then when lust hath conceived, it bringeth forth sin;
and sin, when it is finished, bringeth forth death.
(James 1:13–15)

Naomi complained out of desperation—a place of no hope—because she focused on her own limitations and hardships for a season. She took her focus off God. She wasn't always that way, and let us not judge her. Let's be grateful she's someone to whom we can relate because God later used Naomi to give sound, godly advice to Ruth, leading them to redemption, prosperity, and more!

Naomi's story continues as they returned to Bethlehem during the barley harvest. (Ruth 1:22) Ruth told Naomi she would glean in the fields after the reapers and gather what was left behind. She happened to glean in the field of one of Elimelech's relatives, Boaz, a wealthy man who took notice of Ruth. He protected her by telling the young men in the field not to touch her. He told her to reap in his fields only and to get water when she needed it. He invited her to eat with him, and he told the reapers to drop extra for her to glean. (Ruth 2:2–16)

> *Then she fell on her face, and bowed herself to the ground, and said unto him, Why have I found grace in thine eyes, that thou shouldest take knowledge of me, seeing I am a stranger? And Boaz answered and said unto her, It hath fully been shewed me, all that thou hast done unto thy mother in law since the death of thine husband: and how thou hast left thy father and thy mother, and the land of thy nativity, and art come unto a people which thou knewest not heretofore. The Lord recompense thy work, and a full reward be given thee of the Lord God of Israel, under whose wings thou art come to trust.*
> *(Ruth 2:10–12)*

And by saying all of this, Boaz comforted and encouraged Ruth:

Then she said, Let me find favor in thy sight, my lord; for that thou has comforted me, and for that thou has spoken friendly unto thine handmaid, though I be not like unto one of thine handmaidens.
(Ruth 2:13)

She must have been exhausted after the journey to Bethlehem, after working all day in the fields, and she may have been still grieving the loss of her own husband. She wanted to be a blessing to Naomi, and that's why she worked in the fields to provide for them.

This was not by chance because God was directing Ruth's and Naomi's steps. He was also moving in the heart of Boaz. Naomi's spirit was lifted when she saw how much Ruth had gleaned and knew it could only be by the grace of the Lord. (Ruth 2:18–20)

When Ruth told Naomi all that had happened, Naomi praised God for not forsaking them. She knew Boaz was a close relative who could redeem and provide for them. Naomi instructed Ruth to do what Boaz had told her through the end of the barley harvest. When that time came, Naomi encouraged Ruth differently:

Then Naomi her mother in law said unto her, My daughter, shall I not seek rest for thee, that it may be well with thee?
(Ruth 3:1)

Here we see Naomi the pleasant comforter because she wanted to help Ruth have a better life than working in the fields. Naomi told her to:

Wash thyself therefore, and anoint thee, and put thy raiment upon thee, and get thee down to the floor: but make not thyself known unto the man, until he shall have done eating and drinking. And it shall be, when he lieth down, that thou shalt mark the place where he shall lie, and thou shalt go in, and uncover his feet, and lay thee down; and he will tell thee what thou shalt do. And she said unto her, All that thou sayest unto me I will do.
(Ruth 3:3–5)

Naomi's instruction was a way for Ruth to be humble before Boaz to show she wanted to be covered and protected by him; this touched him deeply because he was older and knew she could have chosen a younger man. It was something he acted upon. He went before the elders at the gate and redeemed Ruth and her late husband Mahlon's property. Boaz became Ruth's husband who also provided for Naomi.

And the women said unto Naomi, blessed be the Lord, which hath not left thee this day without a kinsman, that his name may be famous in Israel. And he shall be unto thee a restorer of thy life, and a nourisher of thine old age: for thy daughter in law, which loveth thee, which is better to thee than seven sons, hath born him.
(Ruth 4:14–15)

Yes, the book is titled after Ruth, but it all started with Naomi. She had been so comforting to Ruth that Ruth made the choice to follow Naomi and her faith. After a period of duress, loss, and complaints, Naomi and Ruth were both comforted and blessed by God, and the blessings were evident to all who saw and knew them. Moreover, Boaz and Ruth had a son named Obed who was the father of Jesse, the father of the holy anointed King David, and in the lineage of Jesus Christ.

TAKEAWAYS

- Even during the longest, hardest storms in our lives, we MUST keep our eyes on the Lord. When we focus on our own abilities, we limit our possibilities.

- God uses our storms to draw us back to Him, yet it's *still* our choice to return. Naomi made that choice, and she was blessed far beyond what she could ever have imagined.

study questions

Where do you think Elimelech was spiritually when he made the decision to move his family away from Bethlehem?

_____

_____

_____

_____

_____

Who do you think made the worst decision in this story: Elimelech or Orpah?

_____

_____

_____

_____

_____

Why?

_____

_____

_____

_____

_____

What happened to revive Naomi back to her pleasant, positive mindset?

_____

_____

_____

_____

_____

chapter 6
FAITHFUL OR FOOLHARDY?
ABIGAIL AND NABAL

Faithful:
Acting with care, loyalty, and allegiance

Foolhardy:
Behaving foolishly; bullheaded or headstrong;
without thought or care

During the Depression Era, many people "scraped by" financially (as the saying goes), so it was not really uncommon for couples to marry with only a few dollars in their pockets. At least that's how my grandparents began their union. In those days, people didn't have much, but they knew how to work hard. They had to! After a few years, my grandparents finally saved enough money to open a small grocery store. My grandfather was a trained butcher and ran the fresh meat section while my grandmother supervised the rest of the store and handled the bookkeeping. Life was finally becoming prosperous for them, and they were also blessed with two little girls: my mother and my aunt, followed some years later by my uncle.

Life was great! They were respected by people in their hometown, and their family was healthy. But troubles have a way of shouldering their way in suddenly, and my grandfather discovered his little haven was certainly not immune to the storm headed their way. There was no way of stopping it or shielding themselves from the news that would change the plans they had for their future.

My grandparents' reaction was one of shock when they learned my grandfather was called into active duty during WWII. It was questionable to many in their small town as to why he was even called at his age—and with a family. He was given a very short time to report for duty, and as a result, my grandparents had only a few weeks to get ready to move. They had no option but to sell their business, which they had to let go for considerably less than it was worth. Someone else ultimately benefited from their long hours of hard work. There was no time to complain or hardly breathe…only to move forward as my grandfather was called to serve his country.

It was exhausting and frightening for my grandmother: She traveled several days by train—protecting her little girls—in order to meet my grandfather already stationed in California. She left the security they had built and decided to trust in a greater purpose ahead.

Though times were troublesome for most Americans, it was still a period of unity. My grandparents spoke of how they made new friendships, cooked for people, and rebuilt their lives serving our country. They didn't have much but were givers anyway. They moved temporarily in a home they shared with multiple people who loved "Chris's fried chicken." This new "storm" became a journey much like the streets they traveled while in San Francisco: There were highs and lows, ups and downs. Years later, my grandfather told me that if it were not for the sale of the business and his call to serve our country, he might not have ever given his heart over to Jesus Christ. You see, he was a religious, lost person, and there was his blessing for being faithful, even when he didn't understand the storm.

It's our responsibility to do our duty. It's important to be known as people who stand true to their word and to do what's right. But that's not true for all people.

In the Bible, there is a short story of a man named Nabal who was considered great due to his wealth and possessions. He had 3,000 sheep and a thousand goats (1 Samuel 25:2–3) and was of the lineage of Caleb. Now Caleb is famously depicted in scripture—along with Joshua—for having big enough faith to believe the Israelites could overtake Canaan as God promised. In fact, many people remember Joshua more than Caleb, but it was Caleb who first had the fortitude and faith to overcome what seemed impossible:

And Caleb stilled the people before Moses, and said,
Let us go up at once, and possess it; for we are well able
to overcome it.
(Numbers 13:30)

Twelve men representing the Jewish tribes spent forty days spying out the land in Canaan only to return and declare "we were in our own sight as grasshoppers, and so we were in their sight." (Numbers 13:33) They were correct in their opinion because there were giants in the land. There were numerous tribes of mighty men surrounding Canaan in the land, the mountains, and by the sea. Yes, the land was fruitful, and the spies brought back proof of that: figs, pomegranates, and grapes. (Numbers 13:23) It was their lack of faith, though, that they brought back as well, and this ultimately affected the Jews for generations.

Caleb: Here was a fearless, faithful, wise man chosen by Moses to represent the tribe of Judah (Numbers 13:6)—the tribe of our Lord Jesus Christ—whom years later would have a rich relative with no concern for doing what is right in the sight of the Lord. Caleb in Hebrew means "whole hearted," but Nabal means "fool."

Wealth is a funny thing. We all wish for it, and we need it to provide for our families, but it can prevent us from being all God wants us to be. Wealth can take our minds off Christ as being our Provider. Wealth can give us a false sense of security. Wealth can make us feel more important than we really are. In reality, the Lord blesses with wealth to provide for our families and to enable us to be a blessing to others.

Wealth doesn't prevent storms from coming into our lives, though, and it certainly doesn't assure us of our good health and survival.

The story continues stating that David and his men had just experienced a life-changing encounter with King Saul where David showed extreme mercy and refused to take King Saul's life when he had opportunity. It was where they were all in a cave, and David cut off Saul's skirt while he was sleeping. (1 Samuel 24:4) Although David regretted it, it proved David could have killed Saul while he slept. It was an eye-opening moment for Saul because he realized David would become king. So they each went their own way, and this led David eventually to the wilderness of Paran (1 Samuel 25:1), as Saul would still pursue David's life.

It was here David and his six hundred men who admired and followed him kept peaceful watch with shepherds and their flocks belonging to the man named Nabal. The men did no harm to anyone. They probably procured their own food and water, asking nothing of nor stealing from the shepherds. (1 Samuel 25:7) All they did was protect them and have friendly conversations. Then, David heard that Nabal was shearing his sheep—or reaping his harvest. Because of this, David sent ten of his men to ask for part of the harvest in exchange for their protection they had provided, which made it possible for Nabal to have his "harvest" and his riches. But trouble came along during that season of reaping, and it could have been prevented.

Though wealthy, Nabal was a mean, drunken man, known as wretched and not one to keep his word. Though in the lineage of

Caleb, he did not follow after God. David instructed his men to greet Nabal and his household in peace (1 Samuel 25:5–6) and basically treat him with respect and to do no harm. Just because they were living in the wilderness didn't mean they couldn't show respect and exhibit good manners. I'm sure their mothers had taught them right!

But Nabal had no insight because he was foolish. He must have known his flocks were protected or he would not have had the great number he had during shearing time. We know this because even his own shepherds spoke on the men's behalf. (1 Samuel 25:14–15) Nabal, though, showed no respect to David and his men and even demeaned him—pretty much calling him a runway servant:

> *And Nabal answered David's servants, and said, Who is David? and who is the son of Jesse? there be many servants nowadays that break away every man from his master. Shall I then take my bread, and my water, and my flesh that I have killed for my shearers, and give it unto men, whom I know not whence they be?*
> *(1 Samuel 25:10–11)*

Everyone at that time had heard of David. In fact, that is the reason King Saul was so jealous of David and wanted to murder him. Crowds of people were saying Saul had killed his thousands, but David had killed his ten thousands. (1 Samuel 18:7–8) David was so popular they wrote a song using these lyrics. One might believe a famous song writer would probably pen a number one hit about David, and everyone would know the lyrics and sing along every time the song came on the radio.

Literally everybody had heard of David and his men. Nabal absolutely without a doubt had heard of David, yet he had no fear or respect for him. More than likely, Nabal was a supporter of King Saul. It brings to mind politics of today. It doesn't matter which group says what, neither is going to be happy with the other's credentials or fanfare unless it benefits their own cause.

Nabal foolishly believed he was great in his own eyes, and he didn't see the storm that was brewing caused by his own actions.

Instead of being grateful for David's protection, he griped about even the thought of sharing his harvest with David and his men. (1 Samuel 25:11) This offended David who needed the food for his soldiers, so he made plans to kill Nabal and his household out of vengeance. He gathered four hundred of his men while two hundred remained with their other belongings—their "stuff." (1 Samuel 25:13) Bet you didn't know the word "stuff" was in the Bible!

I believe what happened next is that Nabal bragged how he put David and his men in their place, which he thought was very low. He bragged to his shepherds and to his servants. He started planning a feast fit for a king. (1 Samuel 25:36)

After his sheep were sheared, he didn't dedicate anything as an offering to the Lord. He didn't set aside any portion for the less fortunate. Instead, he created a huge celebration with himself as the main guest.

While Nabal was boasting and making his lofty plans, a good-hearted, young shepherd slipped away and informed Abigail of what had just happened. This indicates Nabal's servants even thought of him as foolish, because even this young man had heard of David, and knew he and his men would probably come after Nabal and his household. Mind you HE didn't want to be part of the "ten thousands" sung about in the now-famous lyrics.

This is when the young man assured Abigail that David and his men had neither harmed nor stolen from them; he confirmed their friendly conversations and the fact they had been "a wall" (1 Samuel 25:15–16) protecting them in the day and night. What was the problem? As head of his house, Nabal spoke for everyone—including his servants—and they would all suffer the consequences of Nabal's foolish behavior.

The brave, young servant thought differently of Abigail, though. Her name in Hebrew means, "My father is joy." She was a beautiful woman who was intelligent, understanding and discerning. (1 Samuel 25:3) She must have been a good listener and had excellent rapport with people. There's no telling how many times Abigail had already intervened for Nabal's foolish remarks and decisions; it could have been common occurrence or else the servant may not have had the confidence to go to her in the first place. He could have run away or run after David's men himself to make his plea. Instead, he went to Abigail with the assurance she could and would fix the problem. In other words, he had faith in Abigail because she already had a track record.

Now therefore know and consider what thou wilt do;
for evil is determined against our master, and against
all his household; for he is such a son of Belial, that a
man cannot speak to him.
(1 Samuel 25:17)

Maybe the young servant heard David's men talking as they left. More than likely, David's testimony was enough for the servant to know something bad was going to happen to Nabal and the entire household. In fact, he was right! David was furious at Nabal's actions and words and vowed to kill everything belonging to Nabal. (1 Samuel 25:21–22)

The servant referred to Nabal as "master," but he also referred to him as a "son of Belial." According to biblestudytools.com, this was a common expression used in the Old Testament to mean "worthless and wicked." In the New Testament it references Satan. The young servant had no fear of calling his master that degrading expression in the face of his mistress. I believe this shows familiarity, like, "Uh...Mrs. Abigail? Um...Mr. Nabal is at it again! He's gone off and run his foolish mouth, but this time he did it to the wroooooong person!!"

To support this premise, Abigail didn't even question the validity of this strong accusation! She immediately set into action gathering food:

Then Abigail made haste, and took two hundred
loaves, and two bottles of wine, and five sheep ready
dressed, and five measures of parched corn, and a

> *hundred clusters of raisins, and two hundred cakes of*
> *figs, and laid them on asses.*
> *(1 Samuel 25:18)*

Abigail knew how to handle the problem that her foolish husband had caused. She sent her servants on ahead because there was no time to waste. Four hundred angry, hungry men were racing their way. Maybe she stopped to change her clothes to be presentable after the rush of gathering the food. She would need all the leverage she could get because she was about to meet David head on in a desperate plea for the life of all associated with Nabal.

Abigail had big faith as indicated that she didn't run away to save herself. She put her own life on the line when she hopped on the donkey that took her on the road where she came face-to-face with David and his men. When she saw him, she immediately jumped off and bowed herself low in his presence.

> *Let not my lord, I pray thee, regard this man of Belial,*
> *even Nabal: for as his name is, so is he; Nabal is his*
> *name, and folly is with him: but I thine handmaid*
> *saw not the young men of my lord, whom thou didst*
> *send. Now, therefore, my lord, as the Lord liveth, and*
> *as thy soul liveth, seeing the Lord hath withholden thee*
> *from coming to shed blood, and from avenging thyself*
> *with thine own hand, now let thine enemies, and they*
> *that seek evil to my lord, be as Nabal. And now this*
> *blessing, which thine handmaid hath brought unto*
> *my lord, let it even be given unto the young men that*
> *follow my lord. I pray thee, forgive the trespass of thine*

handmaid: for the Lord will certainly make my lord a
sure house; because my lord fighteth the battles of the
Lord, and evil hath not been found in thee all thy days.
(1 Samuel 25:25–28)

- The verses revealed Abigail's wisdom and strong faith in the Lord.

- She showed reverence to the Lord multiple times while also addressing David as her master or lord.

- She reminded him that he is a servant to the Most High King.

- She clarified that the Lord is protecting him and not allowing him to make a mistake by killing Nabal's innocent family and servants.

- She acknowledged her husband was a fool, so in other words, he wasn't worth it!

- She reminded David that he fights God's battles, and God blesses him for that.

- She also said she had not been aware of the conversation Nabal had with David's men, but would he please forgive *her* anyway!

- She identified herself as a supporter by saying David was fighting on behalf of the Lord, which was contrary to what Nabal had said.

- She was begging for the life of everyone in her household, even the servants.

- Abigail gathered food and beverage, and threw herself at David's feet.

- She asked David to overlook foolish Nabal and his ways and put the offense on *her*!

In other words, Nabal's foolish decision was not worth David's act of vengeance. Abigail was encouraging David to let God handle it. What great advice framed in an attitude of humbleness! What wisdom! She was definitely the opposite of her husband's character. The book of James shows how Abigail got her faith and wisdom:

> *If any of you lack wisdom, let him ask of God, that giveth to all men liberally, and upbraideth not; and it shall be given him. But let him ask in faith, nothing wavering. For he that wavereth is like a wave of the sea driven with the wind and tossed.*
> *(James 1:5–6)*

Abigail had probably long been battling hardships caused by Nabal, so that when the biggest storm of her life arrived, she immediately stepped into faith action. Actually, faith requires action!

While Abigail called her husband out on his character, she wasn't complaining; she was taking actions to correct the mistake! She knew Nabal was wrong, and she'd probably been in that position before of correcting his mistakes. On the contrary, she could have supported Nabal or even dismissed David's threat, especially if she had been living the same lifestyle as Nabal.

- Nabal was a fool who couldn't even see his impending storm, which he had caused.

- He was selfish and spiritually blind to the need of others even when he was in a position to help.

- Nabal sought happiness in unhealthy forms (gluttony, drunkenness, foulness, power, wealth, etc.).

- He didn't see any need to look to God, yet the Bible tells us clearly, "The fool hath said in his heart, There is no God…" (Psalm 14:1)

Abigail was a wise, discerning woman willing to give even her life when she took to the road looking for David. She had no idea what her fate would be, only that she had to try to defuse his anger. She would give what was rightfully David's and would attempt to give it even if she were killed while trying to make amends.

When Abigail returned home exhausted, she found Nabal drunk at his own party. He even started eating and celebrating without his wife! Did he even wonder where she was? Why didn't he wait for her? It makes one wonder who was even there with him! He was so selfish he didn't even care about his own wife.

So, there she found her husband gorging on a huge feast and drunk out of his foolhardy mind. She was so disgusted that she turned and left him where she found him. She said not a word to him (1 Samuel 25:36) because she knew he was in no condition to hear her, understand her, or even remember what she was going to say. Just as he was unaware how God was working in his wife's life, he was similarly drunkenly oblivious to the storm that had just subsided and spared his own. For the moment.

The following day when Nabal was sober, Abigail told him what happened and how close "he" had come to death. Certainly, it was his own death he was more concerned with than how his actions almost affected everyone else. Reality then whipped out her hand and slapped Nabal in his fleshly, stunned face. It was the last expression he would ever make. The Bible states his heart "died within him, and he became as a stone," which was very likely a stroke or maybe a heart attack. (1 Samuel 25:37) Nabal then suffered ten days before the Lord struck him dead.

When David heard of Nabal's death, he praised God for protecting him from doing wrong; he then met with Abigail and asked her to be his wife [Saul gave his daughter Michal to David, albeit Saul took her back from him in anger and gave her to Paltiel son of Laish (1 Samuel 25:44)]. David respected Abigail because of her good sense, her strong faith in the Lord, and for keeping him from murdering Nabal. She found favor with him and with God.

In the end, Abigail was rewarded with a better life than she had with Nabal—or would have ever experienced with him. Scripture tells us she "hasted, and arose" (1 Samuel 25:42) to go to David to become his wife. She was excited and didn't look back. Yet, if not for her daily faithfulness that prepared her for the biggest storm of her life, the story would be different.

How will your story end?

TAKEAWAYS

- We must be faithful to seek God's face for wisdom, which will prepare us for life's storms.

- Abigail knew Nabal had sinned, yet humbled herself and asked David to place Nabal's sins upon her. Christ came to earth as a sinless man and gave His life so we can have eternal life through Him.

- "A good name is rather to be chosen than great riches, and loving favour rather than silver and gold." (Proverbs 22:1)

study questions

What type of father and mother do you think Abigail had?

_____

_____

_____

_____

_____

_____

Why do you think they permitted her to marry Nabal?

_____

_____

_____

_____

_____

Do you think they knew of Nabal's bad testimony and character?

_____

_____

_____

_____

_____

_____

How can we remain more steadfast in our faith when we are surrounded by faithless people?

_____

_____

_____

_____

_____

Abigail was in an unequally yoked marriage. What does her storm and how she handled it say about Abigail?

_____

_____

_____

_____

_____

Nabal lived with a God-fearing woman. What does this say about him?

_____

_____

_____

_____

_____

_____

What influence do you think Abigail had on those in Nabal's household? This was a major life storm for them as well.

_____

_____

_____

_____

_____

_____

chapter 7

FRUITFUL OR FORGOTTEN?

JOSEPH

> **Fruitful:**
> Productive; producing helpful results
>
> **Forgotten:**
> Not noticed inadvertently

During the years when so much was collapsing around our family, I was offered a job at our church's Christian academy. Previously, I had been a director of public relations and development for ten years at a homeless rescue mission where my husband was also the director of ministries. Following that, we owned a successful business for ten years. I was taking a few years off to homeschool our two younger children, and it was during this seemingly pinnacle period when a large storm came along busting up all our dreams.

Needing work, I was hired full time and given the opportunity to create a public relations department two days a week in an office I shared with the bus ministry and the coffee pot. This turned out to be a blessing because I built friendships with people who came in, chatted, and prayed with me. I was encouraged.

The other three days of the week I was assigned to teach credit recovery courses. My classroom was a tiny, chocolate brown block room in the farthest corner of the back building on campus. The one small window I had was decorated with a single, country blue curtain that when pulled aside, perfectly framed my view of the church cemetery. Wonderful. Dreadful. Three-fifths of my weekly responsibilities—and the location—were not any positions to which I had aspired. While I enjoyed my time with the students, I found myself asking God if He had forgotten me...us...my family.

I was extremely grateful for the ministry position, but the pay didn't even cover our basic bills. And I mean basic. It was such a difficult time. Why did He have me where I was? Why did we have to lose so much after working so hard for it? Had we done something and caused Him to turn His back on us? Was He ashamed of me? Had I displeased Him? Was He angry at me? Had He forgotten us?

I recall going into town one day out of necessity and trying to rush in and out of a store. It happened that an acquaintance of my precious mother who had recently passed stopped me, squinted her eyes together as she looked me up and down, and asked, "Virginia? Is there something wrong? Are you okay?"

Some may think this was asked out of concern, but I knew by her expression she was referring to my appearance. Yes, I *was* different. I had changed and even carried myself differently. I knew it. I remember a friend of mine asking me one day, "Where is Virginia?" She reminded me of what I had accomplished in my past: pageant titles, a full scholarship to a university, business awards and recognitions. She was right. "Where was Virginia?"

It was about that time when I realized I needed to pursue a dream that had been in my soul for years: I had a calling to write about what God was doing in my life. I had already put my heart to work at the academy where people considered me a leader. I had always had a knack to lead but never really tried to position myself in that role. But I was in a different place in life now. I was broken, yet here I was chosen the PTO president for numerous years. My heart was crushed, but I knew God led me to raise money for gym flooring, a scoreboard, student scholarships, and much more. I was exhausted emotionally and physically, yet my God chose to use me where I was! Cemetery view and all!

Pardon, but "Me, me, me" had gotten old.

I had to first stop asking God, "Why me?" and realize God was *in* all the chaos. The storm. The losses. I mean, He was right there in the gains. I knew God had a purpose for me and decided to work and pray hard where He had me. I knew God needed me to be there. I helped students grow, and I helped the academy grow, and I grew spiritually.

One day I looked out through the tiny window and noticed a beautiful, tall oak tree. It had been there all along! And just beyond the tree sat the original white-frame church built in the 1800s. I paused as I realized I had been missing the beauty that was right in front of me. What a revelation!

Interestingly enough, it was this very setting that formed the foundation my husband and I needed to understand the workings of the academy. It was during those years behind the scenes God grew us to be able to step up into leadership positions in the coming years to help preserve the academy and ministry.

God always had a plan.

My surroundings were what I made of them, and I had allowed the view from within and without to mirror my circumstances. The cemetery was not my prison; my mind and my heart were.

During these years, Joseph's story in the Bible blessed my heart in many ways. Joseph is a hero of mine—someone whom I aspire to be on many levels.

Joseph's story really begins with his father, Jacob, whose name was changed in Genesis 32 from *supplanter*, meaning "to trip up or over throw" or "holder of the heel" to *Israel*, which means "wrestles with God" or "triumphant with God." Jacob had run away from home in fear of his life two decades prior to where we are going to begin this story.

Jacob was told of God to return to his homeland Canaan after serving his father-in-law Laban (a Syrian) for twenty hard years. Laban treated Jacob dishonestly many times throughout the years by making him serve seven years in order to marry Rachel, only to have Laban switch to Leah on the wedding night. Laban then made Jacob serve another seven years for Rachel, the woman he really loved. Laban also changed Jacob's salary ten times and made him work another six years for the cattle. Jacob even believed in his heart that Laban would have sent him away completely empty-handed if it had not been for God and a fear of his brother-in-law Isaac. (Genesis 31:41–42)

It was this return trip, though, when Jacob was going to face his greatest fear: his twin brother, Esau, patriarch of the Edomites. The story has been told many times of how Jacob grabbed the heel of Esau during childbirth, seemingly in an effort to not allow Esau the birthright. It is also well-known that Jacob took advantage of Esau during a weak moment after hunting and made him promise to give over the birthright for a bowl of red pottage (lentil stew). This is why Esau's descendants became known as Edomites, which means "red" in Hebrew. (Genesis 25:27–34)

This birthright was of most importance because it determined who would be head over the family and the possessions. He would receive a double-blessing portion and would have a special covenant relationship with the Lord. (Genesis 27) Isaac loved Esau, but Rebekah favored Jacob, so she deceitfully plotted with Jacob in order to get all of the blessings of the birthright, which is what happened...and then Jacob ran for his life.

So, the "supplanter" ended up having a difficult future, yet he had God's hand of protection on him. (Genesis 31:42) There is much depth to this story, but suffice it to be written that Esau completely forgave Jacob of his theft and wrongdoing and welcomed him back home. This forgiveness was a great surprise and relief to Jacob, who had approached Esau in complete humbleness with gifts and offerings.

This is definitely a story of forgiveness and redemption that must have been shared many times in both families as they were drawing water, watching the flocks, or sitting by the fires at night. It is highly probable this story was passed on to Jacob's sons—and Joseph must have tucked it away in his heart.

Something to note is that Jacob still possessed the birthright. What happened to Esau is that he determined both of their families were so blessed with possessions that the land wasn't big enough for both of them. In Genesis chapter 36, we learn Esau moved his family to Mount Seir, and Jacob's family remained in Canaan—God's blessed land for the Jews.

History has a way of repeating itself sometimes, and Jacob now found himself in a similar situation as his father, Isaac: he had a favorite son. Joseph was very special to him because he was the son of his beloved Rachel. Sadly, Rachel died after an especially hard labor when she gave birth to her child, Benjamin, on their journey back to Canaan.

This favoritism didn't prevent Joseph from working hard like his brothers; he also worked in the fields tending to the flocks.

(Genesis 37:2) This was not always the case as indicated in Genesis 37:12–14 when he remained at home with his father while his brothers went to feed the flocks in Shechem. Maybe he was home one particular day because his father wanted to spend time with him, but a storm of resentment was building because the siblings had long known of Joseph's special treatment:

Jacob placed Rachel and Joseph last in the caravan when they returned to Canaan just in case Esau chose to harm his family. The handmaidens—or secondary wives—and their children went first, followed by Leah and her children, then came Rachel. Leah's children and the children of Bilhah (Rachel's maid) and Zilpah (Leah's maid) were older and may have known why they were positioned earlier in the caravan. For certain, the wives knew and may have talked about it through the years. (Genesis 33:1–2)

Jacob made Joseph a coat of many colors. Dyes were valuable, so this was an important coat that called for attention and indicated importance. None of the other children were presented with such a coat because they probably wore customary shepherd's clothing: dull and natural in coloring. Note: More than likely, the coat and shepherd's clothes were made of one material because Deuteronomy 22:11 forbids unequal "yoking": "Thou shalt not wear a garment of divers sorts, as of woolen and linen together."

Joseph also had dreams where his brothers and parents would bow down to him (as even interpreted by his father), so this did not set well in building a better relationship with the siblings.

Joseph didn't always have to go work in the fields with his brothers and was sometimes sent to check on them. The brothers may have seen him as a tattle-tale brat.

This favoritism came to a head the day Joseph went to check on his brothers on behalf of his father. He chose that day to wear his special coat and of course was seen far off because of such vibrant colors in contrasting the landscape of vast browns and greens.

The brothers resented him so much that their anger and jealousy turned into a murderous plot. Ultimately, he was not killed but thrown into a pit, then sold into slavery for twenty pieces of silver. He was sold once again when the Ishmaelite merchants sold him to Potiphar, one of Pharaoh's officers in Egypt. (Genesis 37:28–36)

Joseph was seventeen years of age.

This famous story continues as Joseph serves in Potiphar's home with God's hand upon him and blessing all he does. Joseph was so successful with everything he handled in Potiphar's home that all responsibilities and decisions were eventually left to Joseph to handle. Potiphar didn't even know what he owned or had, except what he was eating when he sat down at the table. (Genesis 39:6) His trust in Joseph was amazing! It was then that Joseph was pursued by Potiphar's wife, wrongly accused of trying to be intimate with her, and ultimately imprisoned for a lie. (Genesis 39:7–20)

Joseph came from a wealthy, blessed family—a favored son— only to be forsaken by his brothers and possibly forgotten by his father (maybe he thought so initially since Jacob didn't look for him because he was told Joseph was dead). He was falsely accused and now incarcerated. He was so low, the pit his brothers had thrown him in after they ripped off his beautiful coat probably seemed like only a dream.

Joseph may have felt forgotten, but he was so much more than that! God's favor was still upon Joseph even while in prison, so let's try to visit there.

It's likely Joseph served during the Middle Kingdom of Egypt, possibly under Sesostris II and Sesostris III. We know being in prison was a serious matter just like today but with a swifter sentencing period. According to a paper written by Dr. Charles Aling in *Bible and Spade,* prisoners were awaiting their fates of either death or freedom. A good example was the story of the butler and the baker who were imprisoned. The baker was put to death for his offense, but the butler was redeemed by Pharaoh only to then forget Joseph, who remained imprisoned for two more years. The Aling paper brings up an interesting theory: the fact that Joseph was still in prison may indicate Potiphar's question over his wife's accusation.

The Aling paper also indicates that because he was educated, Joseph may have been a scribe when he was promoted to a higher position of authority. Whatever he did, we know he eventually ran the prison.

Still, it was a prison and not a high-rise, window-encased corporate building with a cafeteria and employee gym. It was a dark place. Genesis 41:14 clearly describes it was a "dungeon."

Rats were probably unwelcome cell mates and shared prisoners' meals. The prisoners were dirty, smelly, and unshaven; in fact, Joseph was brought up in a hurry to change his clothes and to shave before he could be presented to Pharaoh. The Aling paper states a bearded face was not accepted in Egypt, and that is one of the reasons he had to shave. Can you imagine the stench? Joseph no longer looked like the seventeen-year-old Joseph: sweat-filled rags replaced his colorful coat of prominence. His skin and nails were stained from his dirty surroundings and lack of running water and facilities. His hair was uncombed, matted, and long. His face was beginning to show stress lines around his eyes. He was older and even had a grown-man's beard.

Joseph was in charge of the prison, but he was still a prisoner.

There, Joseph had a lot of time to reminisce. He thought of all the little sheep he tended for his father. Maybe he recalled a day when he heard the bleating of a little lost lamb and went out and rescued it. Stories his father told him came flooding into his mind at night as he lay curled trying to warm himself. He may have thought back to when he turned thirteen—a coming-of-age period for a young Jewish boy—when Jacob shared how much he loved his wife, Rachel but Laban stole his sacred marriage night. Maybe Jacob even divulged, among other things, how God blessed and protected him in spite of how unfairly Laban treated him in business.

We know he wasn't considering vengeance because Joseph could not have been fruitful or found favor during his storm if he were dwelling on negative thoughts and desires. The lessons Jacob taught encouraged Joseph to do right even when he wasn't treated the same—to be fruitful during the storm. This certainly would have encouraged and prepared Joseph for his personal trials that were bound to arise.

For certain, Joseph remembered how much he was loved by his father. It was something Joseph had been told many times, and believed!

One of the biggest storms of Joseph's life was a place where godly instruction aligned with reality and made itself known: for when there's nothing else but stories of God's prevailing hand…there is hope. The Bible is full of those stories.

It was this hope that helped Joseph get up every morning, waking to the stench of filth.

It was this hope that formed a positive attitude noticed by the keeper of the prison.

It was this hope that gave Joseph the desire to work hard and be useful even in prison.

It was this hope that gave Joseph favor.

No longer was Joseph the tattle-tale brat.

The prison guard gave Joseph full leadership of the prison (Genesis 39:23) and didn't even question how or what Joseph was doing because all prospered under him. That made the prison keeper look good while doing nothing! How convenient! Doesn't that remind you of Potiphar?

What else do we know about Joseph's time in prison? Scripture states Joseph remained in prison two years after the butler forgot him. (Genesis 41:1) We know he was thirty years of age when he was finally brought before Pharaoh's presence to interpret the famous dream about the coming famine. (Genesis 41:46) That indicates, therefore, Joseph was a slave and imprisoned for thirteen years in Egypt before being appointed ruler over all Egypt, second only to Pharaoh himself. (Genesis 41:40–41)

During the next seven years, we know Joseph had two sons whose names clearly reveal the mark left on Joseph's heart during those first twenty years:

> *And Joseph called the name of the firstborn Manasseh: For God, said he, hath made me forget all my toil, and all my father's house. And the name of the second called he Ephraim: For God hath caused me to be fruitful in the land of my affliction. And the seven years of plenteousness, that was in the land of Egypt, were ended. And the seven years of dearth began to come, according as Joseph had said: and the dearth was in all lands; but in all the land of Egypt there was bread. (Genesis 41:51–54)*

God blessed Joseph and caused him to be fruitful in a strange land. Though he was comforted, the story wouldn't be complete without stating Joseph was eventually reunited with his father and brothers two years into the famine. Even during the heartbreaking reunion, Joseph was able to see past his painful years and realize

God allowed the storm to provide for the entire family during the years of famine.

> *Now therefore be not grieved, nor angry with yourselves, that ye sold me hither; for God did send me before you to preserve life. For these two years hath the famine been in the land; and yet there are five years, in the which there shall neither be earing nor harvest. And God sent me before you to preserve you a posterity in the earth, and to save your lives by a great deliverance.*
> *(Genesis 45:5–7)*

God is able to make us fruitful during our life storms. When we are living in the center of God's will, we are not forgotten by God when the storms roll. He simply has a greater purpose in mind for us, but we must be fruitful in order to achieve that purpose. Let the storm rise! He is The Calm in the storm!

TAKEAWAYS

- His storm was growing him to becoming a serving, patient leader—a wise man of God.

- Joseph's experience proves we can still be fruitful while going through a life storm.

- It's important to understand and plant firmly in our hearts that injustices can also be part of God's divine plan.

study questions

What do you think Joseph really meant when he said he forgot his father and brothers as stated in Genesis 41:51?

_____

_____

_____

_____

_____

_____

How can you be fruitful right now in the midst of your current storm?

_____

_____

_____

_____

_____

_____

Where should you begin?

_____

_____

_____

_____

_____

What caused Joseph to have God's favor upon his life?

_____

_____

_____

_____

_____

How can you have God's favor on yours? (Read Psalm 37)

_____

_____

_____

_____

_____

chapter 8
BELIEVER OR BLAMER?

JOB

Believer:
A person who believes and has confidence or faith

Blamer:
Someone who places responsibility for an offense or error on someone or something else

It was Thanksgiving 2012, and Christmas was fast approaching. My family was grateful for what we had, but we were still experiencing painful, deep losses that tumbled one after another. While we were weathering major storms that were pushing us to our knees, gusts would come along just to make the fight a little more interesting: The refrigerator broke. The electrical panel on the stove flamed out, scorching the wall behind it and leaving us to cook on a hot plate for nearly a year. We were grateful for that hot plate. The pantry was almost bare, and I found myself watering down the milk to make it go further. Our savings, which we were living off of, was disappearing fast. There was a level of family tension we had never experienced before. Even more personally, I was sinking deeper into grief over my mother's death.

Out of frustration, my husband asked me, "What next?!" And as if on cue, part of the barn's roof blew off during an unexpected storm the very next day.

Well, he *did* ask.

It reminded me of a few years back when we had experienced several major storms. Those losses always left me with this sense of dread, even though I prayed and prayed we would never have to face something like that ever again. I recall my husband even taking me aside one day to discuss what we had nested away as precaution against any hardships or unexpected winds. We had enough. More than enough. God had blessed us in a big way. So why couldn't I exhale? And just when I thought I could, trouble came knocking again, and this time he was breaking down the door.

We knew we were experiencing a Job-like situation, and we prayed it would never reach that frightening place. The book of Job has only forty-two very short chapters. It paints a story that comes from nightmares—the ones that stay in the recesses of your mind and leave you wondering what's around the next corner. It's the story of one man and his wife's loss of their ten children and the home where they were gathered; their livelihood, which was all their oxen, asses, sheep, and camels; and all of their servants except the ones who escaped to tell Job of the tragedies. (Job 1) Later, Job even lost his health and sense of hope. He also lost the respect of everyone around him—who looked upon him with disgust. It is literally the worst thing you can imagine.

I was studying the book of Job during this time, and it took me along on his soul-searching journey to see God in a way he never had before. It was here I found another biblical key to overcoming life storms.

Job. Ever wonder why you have never met any parents who named their children Job? His story is quite famous, and yet no one wishes Job's hardships and trials upon their children. Job brings to mind death and suffering, but the shadow through which he traveled brought him to a closer relationship with the Lord.

He was never the same Job after he experienced the storm of his life. Let's learn about him.

Before his trials came along, Job was a wealthy man with a large family. His ten children were adults and led lives of ease. They had their own homes—at least we know the seven sons did as Job 1:4 tells us. The sons respected and enjoyed their three sisters' company and invited them to their homes when they each hosted a special feast, which would mean seven days of feasting. The children had plenty to eat and wear, were in good health, they got along well together, they had servants to take care of their businesses and work, and they had no worries. They enjoyed celebrating their good fortune.

Job loved his children, and being a God-fearing man, he prayed over them and made offerings to God just in case they had sinned and "cursed God." (Job 1:4–5) Life was good, but still he had a fear it could turn upside down, so he prayed constantly.

He also lived a life of comfort. He had a nice clay home (referred to by Eliphaz in Job 4:19) and plenty of servants. His business dealings were successful. His wife was happy and taken care of, and you know the saying: Happy Wife = Happy Life. He also had friends, and people treated him respectfully because of his success and good nature. The Bible states in Job 1:3 that he "...was the greatest of all the men of the east." He was a good man. He was powerful. And everyone knew of his strong reverence for God.

Job's wife was highly regarded and elevated as a woman for several reasons: Job loved her and believed she stood out from other women as wise. She was blessed with many children, and her husband was highly respected being in a position of authority, wealth, and of good character. These indicated the blessings of the Lord were upon her. She lived in a home with all of her needs met by her husband and her servants. Though nameless in the Bible, we know she must have been proud of Job and his position in society. Sadly, she has long been considered the opposite of an encouraging person, but let me emphasize this: She lost everything too.

By the time Job was covered in boils, she was childless and penniless. She would look out and see her husband sitting covered in ashes, scraping his boils after God allowed Satan to touch him. (Job 2) She wasn't perfect and maybe was depressed. In fact, she ultimately responded to the storm by lashing out in the same way many of us might have if we had stepped into her shoes:

> *Then said his wife unto him, Dost thou still retain thine integrity? curse God, and die.*
> *(Job 2:9)*

The proof that life had been good to them and that he had considered her a wise woman is further evidenced in Job's response to his wife's comment:

> *But he said unto her, Thou speakest as one of the foolish women speaketh. What? Shall we receive good at the hand of God, and shall we not receive evil? In all this did not Job sin with his lips.*
> *(Job 2:10)*

Many of us say things we don't truly mean and wish we could retract once the heat of the moment has passed. Let's try not to judge too harshly. Maybe Job's wife felt helpless and hopeless. Anger usually covers the emotion of fear, which was probably driving her to desperate measures. What future did she and Job have? It must have been devastating to lose her children, her wealth, their position of respect in society, and her husband's health. What kind of future would she have without a husband to provide for her? Maybe she blamed him for their tragedies.

What is evident, though, is *she* was grieving too and *lost sight* of God's purpose in the tragedy.

Job's friends were not much better. News had traveled fast—as bad news usually does—and Eliphaz the Temanite, Bildad the Shuhite, and Zophar the Naamathite discussed the matter amongst themselves and set a time to go meet with their friend Job. By the time they finally arrived, Job had already been "visited" by Satan's wrath. As they traveled, they looked up from a distance and didn't even recognize him. They were so distraught and shocked that they cried for him, tore their clothes, and sat in the ash heap with Job. They started out right, because for seven days and nights they were quiet. But that's hard for many people to do for any length of time: keep quiet. It's so much easier to judge others' problems than to keep silent and be supportive.

But Job broke the silence as he called out in anguish, revealing that his worst nightmare had come to pass:

> *For the thing which I greatly feared is come upon me,*
> *and that which I was afraid of is come unto me. I was*
> *not in safety, neither had I rest, neither was I quiet;*
> *yet trouble came.*
> *(Job 3:25–26)*

See, he always had that nagging feeling life couldn't always be that perfect. You know, that feeling of dread something bad is just around the corner? Or the memory of a terrible dream you had a few nights ago that woke you with sweat dripping from your brow? Yeah, that's the feeling. That's why he prayed constantly as Job 1:5 states. He wasn't taking for granted his blessings from God; he thanked God continually and lifted up intercessory prayers for his children. But trouble came knocking anyway.

Satan had been walking around through the earth and noticed God's favor on Job's life. What Job and his wife didn't know is that God allowed the troubles to come. God was proud of Job. He saw him as a just man and told Satan that, "...there is none like him in the earth, a perfect and an upright man, one that feareth God, and escheweth evil." (Job 1:8)

So, the losses rolled in, leaving Job and his wife childless and penniless. Yet, Job kept his integrity:

> *And said, Naked came I out of my mother's womb, and naked shall I return thither: the Lord gave, and the Lord hath taken away; blessed be the name of the Lord. In all this Job sinned not, nor charged God foolishly.*
> *(Job 1:21–22)*

Back up a little. When Satan visited before God again, God once again claimed precious Job to be an exemplary man:

> *And the Lord said unto Satan, Hast though considered my servant Job, that there is none like him in the earth, a perfect and an upright man, one that feareth God, and escheweth evil? And still he holdeth fast his integrity, although thou movedst me against him, to destroy him without cause.*
> *(Job 2:3)*

But this time, Satan was given permission to touch Job—just not allowed to take his life. Satan chose to clothe Job in boils from the tip of his head to the soles of his feet. And that's the condition Job's friends found him. He was in an ash heap scraping himself with a potsherd—fittingly to our story—which was a broken piece of pottery.

Job still had his house, though, because the Bible states he cried out from his ash heap, "They that dwell in mine house, and my maids, count me for a stranger: I am an alien in their sight." (Job 19:15)

Did Job question why it was happening? Did he feel deserted, alienated by everyone and God? Was his spirit sinking? Was he hurting physically as well? YES! Job didn't believe he had done anything wrong to deserve the hardships.

And then his "friends" began speaking. Eliphaz spoke first and said in chapters 4 and 5 that Job had instructed many people in their troubles, but here he was fainting when hard times fell upon him for the first time. He said people didn't have trouble or perish if they were innocent. He also said, "For wrath killeth the foolish man, and envy slayeth the silly one. I have seen the foolish taking root: but suddenly I cursed his habitation. His children are far from safety, and they are crushed in the gate, neither is there any to deliver them." (Job 5:2–4) He said much more, but this was enough to know he was blaming Job for his own troubles.

Ouch! Thanks, "friend," for reminding Job how his children were crushed under a house and then implying it was his own fault. Job just sank a little deeper into despair.

Bildad the Shuhite spoke next (after Job responded to Eliphaz) and basically said Job was a hypocrite because he considered himself innocent and not worthy of all of the hardships. Among other things, Bildad had this to say:

> *Behold, God will not cast away a perfect man, neither will he help the evil doers: Till he fill thy mouth with laughing, and thy lips with rejoicing. They that hate thee shall be clothed with shame: and the dwelling place of the wicked shall come to nought.*
> *(Job 8:20–22)*

Can you imagine how low Job was feeling at that moment? This is a great example of what not to do when you visit people in need. Sometimes it is best to just sit, listen, and pray with them.

Next up was Zophar who could hardly wait to let Job have a piece of his mind because he got so upset with him. He basically said God had not punished Job as much as he deserved and called him a liar and a hypocrite:

> *Should thy lies make men hold their peace? And when thou mockest, shall no man make thee ashamed? For thou has said, My doctrine is pure, and I am clean in thine eyes. But oh that God would speak and open his lips against thee: And that he would shew thee the*

secrets of wisdom, that they are double to that which is! Know therefore that God exacteth of thee less than thine iniquity deserveth.
(Job 11:3–6)

Well, that did it! Who needs friends like that? Blamers! Condemners! What was the purpose in putting down a man who was already wallowing in an ash heap covered in so many boils that he wasn't recognizable? He must have looked horrible, deformed. Additionally, he was probably not eating, and his hair may have fallen out due to the boils and scraping himself with a sharp instrument. He had lost everything, and now every one of his friends was condemning him.

Where was God? Why didn't He answer Job? He had served God his whole life, so where was God when he needed Him most in the midst of his storm? Job turned to God seeking to find answers. He needed God to respond.

Then, the wind picked up, moving closer, blowing round and round, with the voice of God calling from within:

...the Lord answered Job out of the whirlwind, and said, Who is this that darkeneth counsel by words without knowledge? Gird up now thy loins like a man; for I will demand of thee, and answer thou me. Where wast thou when I laid the foundation of the earth? Declare, if thou has understanding.
(Job 38:1–4)

Job was silent because it became clear that God is Lord over all. He allows what He allows. He created all. Who are we to question Him? There is none greater than the Lord God Almighty. His thoughts are higher than we can even understand.

Job had been serving God from a peripheral viewpoint—like an employee who respects his boss but is afraid of him and keeps busy doing well in his job in the hopes of not being noticed or punished.

Finally, Job had the courage to speak and humbly reply to God's pointed questions:

> *Then Job answered the Lord, and said, I know that thou canst do everything, and that no thought can be withholden from thee. Who is he that hideth counsel without knowledge? Therefore have I uttered that I understood not; things too wonderful for me, which I knew not. Hear, I beseech thee, and I will speak: I will demand of thee, and declare thou unto me. I have heard of thee by the hearing of the ear: but now mine eye seeth thee. Wherefore I abhor myself and repent in dust and ashes.*
> *(Job 42:1–6)*

Job had a good life full of blessings. He had always heard of God and worshiped Him out of reverence and fear. He knew *of* Him, but he now *saw* Him in a different, deeper way. He moved from head knowledge to heart knowledge. God was now real to him like never before. The storms no longer mattered because Job saw

God as sovereign. In fact, Job admitted he couldn't even begin to understand God's ways because they were, "too wonderful" to comprehend.

Instead of ending his life in an ash pit, Job reached up in utter despair, sought God with all he had remaining in his soul, and discovered God in a new way that became personal.

Afterward, the Lord spoke directly to Eliphaz (Job 42:7–9) and admonished him, Bildad, and Zophar for their accusatory, harsh words against Job. They were all wrong because they had not sought God on the matter before they even left together to go see Job, neither when they immediately arrived nor before they spoke to him. To redeem themselves, they were ordered by God to offer a burnt sacrifice, and then their true friend Job would pray for *them*! God then accepted Job and removed the trials when he prayed for his friends.

Job forgave them on the spot because his focus was God. They didn't *have* to blame Job for his troubles. What could and should they have done? If they had sought God, they would have listened quietly as Job spoke of his sorrows. Yes! People need to vent sometimes in confidence with true friends. Could they have offered help? Yes. They could have organized a modern-day "Go-Fund-Me" rally.

God took care of that in the end anyway when He caused people to freely give to Job and his family. In fact, Job and his wife were blessed with twice as much money and cattle as they had prior to their losses—notice his wife was blessed as well, which shows God's beautiful grace. They had ten more children (and the women were the most beautiful in the land). Job lived long enough to see four more generations of his family. (Job 42:12–17)

We should be encouraged to humble ourselves before the Lord, listen to Him, and be willing to hear what God has to say to us. Maybe God has been pleased with you from the beginning, like he was with Job. Maybe, just maybe, God knew all along He could trust you in your trials.

Get to know God in a more intimate way than you ever have before. Seek Him in the storm. Believe God is protecting you. Let God complete the work He has started in you, and you will be blessed.

TAKEAWAYS

- Instead of questioning the storm, seek God's purpose *in* the storm.

- To overcome our life storms, we must have a personal—not a peripheral—relationship with Jesus Christ.

- Always trust that God's plan, even with losses, is greater than any you have planned.

study questions

What do you think Job's friends discussed before they left to visit Job?

_____

_____

_____

_____

_____

_____

Do you think they prayed?

_____

_____

_____

_____

_____

What did Job's friends do right?

_____

_____

_____

_____

What was different about Job after he saw God's sovereignty?

_____

What impact did Job's life storms have on his friends, acquaintances, and family?

_____

chapter 9

COUNSELOR
OR CRITIC?

JESUS

> **Counselor:**
> A person who counsels, advises, or instructs for another person's benefit
>
> **Critic:**
> A person who judges, evaluates, or criticizes

I have decided that social media is not the best place to position myself when I need good counsel. Now, I believe God can use anything or anyone for His glory, but aside from the occasional uplifting memes that cross the social network pages, I personally don't think it's healthy to invest much time there. That decisive moment came the day I read a posting from someone who felt the need to share that she just doesn't have patience or tolerance for people going through hardships.

In contrast, her life is one of success connecting to other successes, so no, she isn't able to empathize with someone who has recently lost a loved one and is feeling depressed, or those who have experienced the uncertainty that comes with losing a job. She's not able to relate to parents who can't afford health care no matter how hard they work or wonder how they are going to feed their family for the next week. Also, looking at someone's third vacation photos in one year knowing that another person can barely fill a gas tank halfway is not something that confirms God's love and blessings of equal value or proportion. That doesn't seem fair, and at best it's not enjoyable. In fact, my heart aches wondering where's the balance of truth among the tweets?

So, while I can be happy for someone who is *viviendo la vida*, I would certainly prefer *not* to seek guidance from someone who had never lived through trials that test character and integrity. I also wouldn't seek out someone who would allow me to stay down in a pit of despair either. I would pray for someone who could relate to my pain and help me move forward to reach my next level through Christ. Someone who could cast a net of compassion or toss me a rope of hope and say, "Here's how God helped me..." or "This scripture helped me..." or even, "Let's pray about it."

The Word of God is alive, you know. It speaks to us when we read. Get quiet. And listen. What I have found to be true is that God Himself is my Deliverer. He is my Provider. He is my Father.

He is my Defender. It was ultimately my alone time with God, in His Word, that changed my heart during my storms. In truth, my reality didn't change much for a while, but my perception of my reality did.

Do you need some of that encouragement to remind you of His love and favor?

1. God's Word says He has good plans for me, so no matter how bad my current situation is, I can be encouraged about my future. That's hope! Just because life may be hard right now doesn't necessarily mean you are being punished. He also allows trials to strengthen us spiritually, to draw us closer to Him, to make us more like Him, to prepare us for a new level in life, and to help fulfill our God-given purpose.

   For I know the thoughts that I think toward you saith the Lord, thoughts of peace, and not of evil, to give you an expected end. (Jeremiah 29:11)

2. God's Word also ensures me that He loves me and brings me to a prosperous place when I am serving Him. We are not assured of what specifically it will be, but it is something comforting and uplifting.

   He brought me to the banqueting house, and his banner over me was love. (Song of Solomon 2:4)

3. Another truth is that we are not promised a smooth ride in life, yet we have victory through Jesus. That's

comforting in itself because it means He has already fought my battles for me and won! This is not our home.

These things I have spoken unto you, that in me ye might have peace. In the world ye shall have tribulation: but be of good cheer; I have overcome the world. (John 16:33)

4. One of the greatest builders up of faith in His Word is the simple truth that even bad times will come around, somehow, to benefit me.

   And we know that all things work together for good to them that love God, to them who are the called according to his purpose. (Romans 8:28)

These are some of God's promises. These are truths.

But there are other truths as well. Storms aren't always a bad thing to happen in life. Think about the sounds of a rainstorm hitting against a roof or a window; some people find this to be very calming. The rain falls breathing in new life and also reviving life that is in jeopardy.

The fact is we need the rain. It's strengthening. It's a life force.

It's not so bad to be in a rainstorm if you are prepared with a raincoat, the proper shoes, an umbrella, or at the very least an unfolded newspaper to hold over your head. So, if we are as prepared as we can be for impending storms, then we can understand this truth: Storms. Eventually. Pass.

No one in the history of the world knew this better than the Man named Jesus, the Son of God who chose to leave Heaven so we might have eternal life through His death. The truth is Jesus experienced every sorrow and pain and therefore can, and does, relate to our desperate times. He is not someone who has no tolerance for our hardships. He understands.

He *is* our Wonderful Counselor. (Isaiah 9:6)

So, now that I have recommended my Counselor to you, let's take a look at a little of His track record.

Jesus is acquainted with grief and sorrow. (Isaiah 53:3) There is a famous story of Lazarus who was raised from the dead, and his miracle is documented in the book of John in Chapter 11. We know Lazarus and his sisters Mary and Martha were close to Jesus's heart because multiple times it is stated how much He loved them and how deeply He was moved by their despair. His love and compassion were so evident that other people noticed it.

There are two facts that are not often linked with this miracle:

1. Jesus was preaching and teaching in Jerusalem when Jews threatened to stone Him to death (John 10:23–39, 11:8), so He and His disciples traveled beyond Jordan for safety. (John 10:40) This is the reason Jesus was not near Bethany where Lazarus lived.

2. Additionally, this is the very miracle that finally led to the plotting of Jesus's death. (John 11:45–57) Jesus knew His

life was in danger if He ever decided to return to any area near Jerusalem, and that included Bethany.

Jerusalem is only about two miles from Bethany. (John 11:18) Lazarus got sick, and his sisters sent for Jesus, knowing He could heal their brother. They were desperate. They appealed to the only One who could help their brother.

> *When Jesus heard that, he said, This sickness is not unto death, but for the glory of God, that the Son of God might be glorified thereby.*
> *(John 11:4)*

At the news of Lazarus's health crisis, Jesus didn't panic. He didn't get up and go immediately to Bethany. He did something unusual that could have been interpreted as indifference: He remained where he was for two more days before telling His disciples that they would go back to Judea. This decision concerned the disciples, but Jesus held firm.

> *These things said he: and after that he saith unto them, Our friend Lazarus sleepeth; but I go, that I may awake him out of sleep. Then said his disciples, Lord, if he sleep, he shall do well. Howbeit Jesus spake of his death; but they thought that he had spoken of taking of rest in sleep. Then said Jesus unto them plainly, Lazarus is dead. And I am glad for your sakes that I was not there, to the intent ye may believe; nevertheless let us go unto him.*
> *(John 11:11–15)*

- Nevertheless, Jesus would follow through, even if others did not believe.

- Nevertheless, He would go to Lazarus and raise him from the dead, even though His life was at stake.

- Nevertheless, Jesus knew His purpose in life and was intent on fulfilling it, even to death.

The account moves forward to the raising of Lazarus even after four days of being dead in the grave. There were many Jews there comforting Mary and Martha. When Jesus raised Lazarus from the dead, it was such a miracle that many people believed Jesus to be the Christ—probably more than if Jesus had healed Lazarus as he lay on his sick bed. It so infuriated the Jewish leaders that they even considered murdering Lazarus too, because of his testimony, which caused many to believe on Jesus. (John 12:10–11)

Later, six days before the Passover, Jesus arrived at Bethany to visit with Lazarus, Mary, and Martha again. This is right before Jesus had His triumphant ride into town while people waved palms in the air shouting with excitement for His arrival. It is just before Mary anoints His feet with spikenard and wipes His feet with her hair.

It is just before Jesus expressed personal despair:

> *Now is my soul troubled; and what shall I say? Father,*
> *save me from this hour; but for this cause came I unto*
> *this hour.*
> *(John 12:27)*

Jesus knew His time was coming near to be crucified. He knew it would not be easy. He prayed for God to save Him from what was definitely going to be terrifying, but He knew His death was vital to the purpose for which He was called.

> *Now is the judgment of this world: now shall the prince of this world be cast out. And I, if I be lifted up from the earth, will draw all men unto me. This he said, signifying what death he should die.*
> *(John 12:31–33)*

Oh, friend, as we conclude it all, we must remember Jesus had critics too. Jesus was hated for doing good, helping people, and pointing people like you and me to God. Jesus experienced the ultimate of criticism as they conspired to capture and kill Him, which led to His spilled blood. Jesus knew there was trouble ahead, but He stepped in the midst of an overcoming story that is still told today. Lazarus's story became more miraculous BECAUSE Jesus delayed the answer. Lazarus's story is still relevant. Jesus's story is always relevant.

Be encouraged in life's delays and seeming declines because God may be planning a bigger, more far-reaching victory than if He had answered your first whispered prayer.

I am praying for you.

TAKEAWAYS

- Trust the Counselor.
- Nothing is too hard for God.
- Jesus understands.
- Trust His timing.

study questions

Has God ever delayed in answering some of your prayers? Did you grow spiritually during that time?

_____

_____

_____

_____

_____

_____

Have you found yourself to be more critical during your life storms or more trusting? What makes the difference?

_____

_____

_____

_____

_____

_____

If God is truly a loving God, why does it seem He doesn't always answer our prayers? Does He?

_____

_____

_____

_____

_____

Have you asked Jesus to be your Counselor, your Savior?

_____

_____

_____

_____

_____

About the Author

Virginia C. Denmark worked in corporate America before entering the ministry serving in public relations and development for a three-campus homeless and recovery center, in private education, and also for their family business. She is a wife, mother, and grandmother.

To author Virginia Denmark, writing this book was a life-long dream that took a lifetime to prepare for. How can you help someone overcome trials if you've never experienced any yourself, right?! In the midst of an extremely trying period, she heeded God's call and wrote a Bible study, which she led at her home church and ultimately became this book.

virginiadenmark.com

WORKS CITED

- Aling, Dr. Charles, "Joseph in Egypt: Part I" in *Bible and Spade*, "Joseph in Egypt: Third of Six Parts," www.biblearchaeology.org.

- www.agapebiblestudy.com/Ruth (Rt 1:22).

- Quayle, Stephen. *Genesis 6 Giants: Israel's War with Giants and Also Giants of Gath*. End Time Thunder Publishers, 2008.

- biblestudytools.com, "son of belial," www.biblestudytools.com/dictionary/belial/